Delore

Meet me at the top. Good luck

Standing In The Shadows Of Greatness

by

Henry J. Pankey

2004

Parkway Publishers, Inc.
Boone, North Carolina

**Henry Pankey is available
for speaking engagements,
and can be reached at:
Phone: (919) 419-8541
Email: eaglehjp@aol.com**

Library of Congress Cataloging in Publication

Pankey, Henry J.
Standing in the shadows of greatness / by Henry J. Pankey.
p. cm.
ISBN 1-887905-94-4
1. Pankey, Henry J. 2. High school principals—United States—
Biography. I. Title.

LA2317.P32A3 2004
371.2′012′092—dc22

2004011985

*Cover Painting by Cynthia Harrell
Cover and Book Design by Aaron Burleson, Spokesmedia
Editing by Julie Shissler*

Dedication

My mother,
Mamie McDuffie Pankey
Because you loved me,
I am what I am.

This book is also dedicated
to my wife, Aleyah
And my children,
Ashia, Amira and Aaron.

Introduction

You must write a book. I would love to read about your life. People want to know this stuff. How did you improve violent, low performing schools? After hearing these types of comments for the last 20 years, I decided that I could no longer put off writing Standing in the Shadows of Greatness.

I was born January 13, 1952 and raised in a small rural southern community in Laurinburg, North Carolina known as Pankey Town. You know the place, but in your town it may be named Washington, Carver, Fredrick Douglas, Lincoln or Martin Luther King, Jr. Yes, we still have the small AME Zion church and folks eat hard fried chicken, collard greens, corn bread, banana pudding, fatback, as well as macaroni and cheese after church on Sundays.

I came into this world with a bald head and I am going out with a bald head.

Although we play the bourgeois game, black folks raised in the south during the 50's lived in a bed of roses complete with the briar patch:

Strong family love and bonding
Seeds of greatness
Hard work
Cotton fields
Tobacco barn
Bleaching cream
Nappy hair
Pig feet
Mosquitoes the size of big beans
Soul music
    Record collection: Otis Redding, James Brown,
    Aretha, Elvis, Righteous Brothers, etc.
Creek liquor
Fish fries
Saying good morning, please, may I, thank you, yes sir
    and no ma'm

Reciting a Bible verse in school each day
Church every Sunday
Laughing at the "saintified" ladies when they got happy
    and shouted
Wigs on sideways
Laughed at old folks with false teeth and hats
Moved when people sat beside you smelling like mothballs
Eating together after church
Doing the nasty behind the house
Everybody eating at the table at the same time
Clean clothes
Skinny-dipping in the stump hole
    (Dog paddling instead of swimming)
Whippings (discipline) with a switch, belt or razor strap
Colored schools
Outdoor toilets
Respect of elders
The slow drag while playing the song Stay in My Corner
Red water pump in the yard
A dog in the back yard
Pigpen
Garden
Photos of John and Jacqueline Kennedy, Martin Luther
    King, Jr. and Jesus Christ in the living room
Coping with racism
First generation to go to college
New millionaires
Proud to be country
Etc.

Although I was tempted to glamorize my childhood, I have come to realize that every hardship represented an extraordinary opportunity to grow, gain insights and get stronger. Behind every adversity was a lesson which put me on the road to understanding that it was all for the best. Standing in the Shadows of Greatness discusses the intangibles of relentless intestinal fortitude solidified by an unconquerable spirit. Plus, all families have problems. All families have successes and failures.

My lifetime achievements entail attending over ten colleges, receiving three college degrees, thirteen licenses in either education or administration, thousands of speaking engagements, hundreds of awards, working as a field hand, cotton picker, bus driver, cook, security guard, typist, teacher, published author, playwright, actor, comedian, impressionists, drug counselor, assistant principal, principal, education consultant and school improvement expert. It is easy to stand tall when you are standing on the shoulders of your ancestors from Pankey Town. Humbly, I recognize that I am a public servant. I am not a perfect servant.

Standing in the Shadows of Greatness is a true testimonial that chronicles the ability of human beings to overcome seemingly unconquerable hardships. It is the truth. Thus, the urban language and experiences are sometimes raw, harsh, but full of hope, determination and inspiration. The human condition is the same all over the world. However, there are differences that we too often ignore. Ignore is the root word of ignorance. The North is not the same as the South. The New York urban school experience is not the same as the rural south or urban schools below the Mason Dixon line. My book will explore and contrast the similarities as well as critical differences between life in New York City and North Carolina.

In 1992, I became principal of Dr. Susan S. McKinney JHS 265 in the Forte Green Projects of Brooklyn, New York. The United Federation of Teachers rated the school the 5th most violent in New York City. New York Newsday spent the first 7 months with me at the school. They took 3500 photographs and interviewed hundreds of the school's stakeholders. In April they wrote a 6-page story that lionized my leadership. WE all know it was a team effort. WE is stronger than ME. Many observers considered the school one of the safest schools in the state.

In 1998, I became principal of Southern High School in Durham, North Carolina. The North Carolina Department of Public Instruction graded the school as one of 11 low performing schools in the state the year before my arrival. Within 4 months the school broke state school improvement records and achieved Exemplary Status at the end of the year. February 22, 2000, US Education Secretary Richard Riley delivered to the nation the 7th Annual State of American Education address from the gym of Southern High School. Southern High School was arguably one of the most improved schools in the United States of America. This historic event was covered by the national media. North

Carolina Governor James Hunt praised the school's leadership. We came to understand, "Not failure, but low aim, is the sin." I made the opening remarks on national television.

Welfare, unemployment, two near death experiences, political bloodbaths, two marriages, character assassination, blistering attacks as well as outstanding support from the newspaper and radio, entanglements with school superintendents and board members, soul searching, blackmail, and extraordinary praise have grounded me with a sincere sense of gratitude and the realization that I wouldn't take nothing for my journey now.

I am fully aware that I have received national recognition as a Tough Love principal and benevolent disciplinarian. Change agents must be tough enough to shoulder criticism. Being an advocate for children is professionally and politically one of the most dangerous missions you can undertake. The love of children is reason enough. I deliberately took assignments in violent, disruptive, low performing schools. I knew the risks. "I ain't mad with nobody. I make no apologies." Tough Love means you don't have to love me back. I tried to make the hard decisions based on love, not toughness. Educators must fight for children because children cannot fight for themselves. All children deserve a school that is either successful or en route to being a success. Schools make far too many decisions based on scores achieved on standardized tests. It is not about tests. It is about saving our children. Children have a lifetime expectancy of 70+ years. Principles are more important than being principal!

Standing in the Shadows of Greatness highlights many of the problems parents, students and professional educators face each day. School improvement strategies are included, but the real heroes are our children. Success is not a mystery. Failure is not an option. Education malpractice is an unacceptable price for a child to pay. We already know all we need to know to successfully teach all children. We also have all the money we need. Teachers have a right to teach and students have a right to learn in a school that is safe, orderly and successful. Schools must meet the needs of all children. All decisions must be made based on what is in the best interest of children.

Greatness and the pursuit of success is the birthright of every child of woman born. Too often, they find themselves at tiptoe stance, on the outside looking in, as they are Standing in the Shadows of Greatness. They need to come out of the shadows and flourish.

Nothing is more important than family. The love of my mother and father, brothers and sisters and strength of my relatives in Pankey Town have more than adequately prepared me for my journey from the cotton fields of North Carolina to the national stage. The unconditional love of my wife, Aleyah, my stepdaughter Ashia Johnson, and my children Amira and Aaron have provided me with formidable strength, faith and vision. Their, support, love, patience, warm and chilling inspiration have fulfilled my life beyond my wildest dreams. "Dream, but don't make dreams your master!"

In essence, ultimately, I want to be able to stand before the great God of the universe and plea for mercy. "Master, I have fought the good fight. I have finished the course and I have kept the faith."

Table Of Contents

"Walk with kings, but keep the common touch."

I've Dreamed Many Dreams

The unkind, coarse, sandpaper of aging has forcibly etched grief-filled memories of pain, suffering, heartache, and disappointment on my mother's bronze face. My father silently stared at the white, wrinkled, and sterilized bed sheets of Scotland Memorial Hospital. His somber silence was indicative of submissive defeatism. The empty hourglass of Gabriel's trumpet was poised to bring the unbearable pain that is death's eternal escort.

Mother, please do not go gently into that unknown, eternal, good night. Fight death. "Yeah, though I walk into the shadows of death" is a soliloquy for another actress on this wretched stage we call earth. Breathe again, speak, sing, and pray, hug, smile, walk, dance, and make some more grits, eggs, bacon and pancakes by the candlelight on the potbellied stove in the ragged, red barn we called home. Remember the words of the anonymous poem that you used to say to me before you put me to sleep:

> I've dreamed many dreams that never came true,
> I've seen them vanish at dawn;
> But I've realized enough of my dreams, thank God,
> To make me want to dream on.
>
> I've prayed many prayers when no answer came,
> I've waited patient and long;
> But answers have come to enough of my prayers,
> To make me keep praying on.
>
> I've trusted many a friend who failed,
> And left me to weep alone;
> But I've found enough of my friends true-blue,
> To make me keep trusting on.

I've sown many seeds that fell by the way,
For the birds to feed upon;
But I've held enough golden sheaves in my hand,
To make me keep sowing on.
I've drained the cup of disappointment and pain,
I've gone many days without song,
But I've sipped enough nectar from the rose of life,
To make me want to live on.

Although the doctors had removed both breasts that nourished me as a baby, my mother was alive. An incision in her smile revealed the umbilical cord between her and sorrow was not broken. Yet the inner walls of her faith, guarded by wisdom, would not stumble, even if the hot ashes from the pits of volcanoes were placed on them. She said, "I am all right. God is still in charge." I knew then, I was Standing In the Shadows of Greatness.

I am who I am because you loved me. I've never told you, I almost drowned in The Graveyard of the Atlantic.

Near Drowning In The Graveyard Of The Atlantic

It was a steamy, sweaty, mosquito-infested, hot, sticky day during the summer of 1969. I was in summer school at the North Carolina School of The Arts. The school had taken a group of us on a field trip to Manteo, North Carolina to see a live theatrical production of The Lost Colony. This was my first time seeing a professional play.

Without permission, my friends and I went swimming. It was a stupid decision. I could not swim and I knew it. Dammit, I was drowning and there was nothing I could do to stop it. My friends, Moses and Robert, were drowning, too. Our other buddy, Harvey, had somehow gotten out of the treacherous waters infamously known as The Graveyard of the Atlantic. Those of us who were drowning were black and could not swim. We were too proud and embarrassed to let our white classmates find out the truth about our inability to match their agility and skills in the ocean.

With impunity, the violent recurring current body-slammed and dropkicked me under the brown reddish muddy waters of Cape Hatteras. Earlier, we had ignored the signs warning, "Do Not Swim in the Area," "Danger: Quick Tides." Mosley was hysterically swinging at the relentless and overpowering waves. My cutup buddy, Robert, was helplessly punching water like a drunken prizefighter.

When I was growing up in Pankey Town, my first cousin, Geneboy, would take me to a mudhole full of water. He taught me to kick and hold my breath while attempting to swim. (Dog paddle is all I knew.) He said to always remember to kick and hold your breath.

My legs grew weary and lost their feeling. I lacked the will or energy to move my arms any more. Suddenly, I saw my funeral at Allen Chapel AME Zion Church in Pankey Town. I smelled embalming fluid and the choking aroma of flowers at my funeral. (No, I did not see a light or travel through clouds.) I sensed the death of fish, oysters, snails, snakes, weeds, worms, lobsters, clams and myself. I became part of everything dead in the ocean. Deep sorrow, regret, guilt, fear, and loneliness were accompanied by the Grim Reaper's visit to my body, spirit, soul, and mind. I was sad because I did not want my mama to see me dead. "My mama gone kill me, if she finds out I drowned."

In crisp, sharp, clear, digital color, I saw my mother crying at my funeral. Her tense, shaking and slumped over body was supported by Aunt Myra and Aunt Carrie Lee. Everybody was crying. My cousins from New York were home. Funerals were big time in the Black communities of the South. Laurinburg's Number One Black undertaker, Bee Morris, had on his black suit and white gloves. He was smiling. Nothing pleases him like a funeral.

I could see my stiff body frozen in a cheap sky-blue casket. The barber, Bernie Jackson, had again cut my hair too short. I never asked him for the Julius Caesar style. I had said a little bit off the top. He always messed up my hair. It doesn't matter what you say, all of his haircuts come out the same way. Ray Charles could do a better job. Bernie would put a bowl on your head and cut away.

Brown powders were on my face. I couldn't move. I tried to yell at Mama. Like the old folks used to say, I was too proud to speak. It was show time! Bigger than Broadway! Hell, this was bigger than Elvis! I had hit the big time and was here for the big show all dressed up in my "Sunday Go to Meeting" cheap, black, polyester suit, hand-me-down white shirt, and clip-on ebony tie!

Gulppp! The hedonistic water violently sledgehammered my chest. It flipped, twisted, tossed and turned me like a pussycat in heat. Breathing became more and more difficult. Sinuses and asthma didn't help.

My first time away from home and my attendance at the N. C. School Of The Arts summer school was the promise of an opportunity to be famous like Sidney Poitier, Bill Cosby, Sammy Davis, Jr. or Harry Belafonte.

The white kids were swimming like Flipper. They had grace, elegance and style. Black folks were kicking up mud in the water. We'd hold our breaths, go under, dog paddle a little...hell, we were fading fast! We had gone too far! Water was over our heads. The tides were powerful and dog paddling didn't help.

Involuntarily, scenes of my childhood were rewinding in my head like an out of control video. Vividly, I began to see little things were of supreme importance. Five cents ice cream. Living in a barn we called home. The smell of tobacco on my daddy's mustache. Remember to polish mama's white nursing shoes. Mama, giving me an alcohol rub, mashed bumps, and killed mosquitoes on my neck. Uncle Johnny was spinning me over his shoulders. God, I wanna live! I want the mystery of death to stay a stranger! God please, I don't wanna be the main attraction at this funeral. Let folks eat chicken and drink creek liquor at another time. This ain't right. I am too young to die!

An angelic voice said to me: "Hanky Panky, you will drown if you don't do exactly as I say. This is Joey. Listen to me. I need you to help me. Relax, lean your head back in the water. Don't fight me. If you fight, I will let you go. Kick with your feet. I'll do the rest. Relax. You are doing good. We got a couple more feet to go........ Now, try to stand up. Can you walk? It's okay. Lay down. It's okay."

The 100-degree sun percolated the salt water as it rolled down my face. Mud scratched my parched testicles. My pants smelled like fish. Maybe I am dead? I rolled my face in the sand. Robert was in a daze, but he was okay. I looked up and saw Mosley vomiting salt water. His body went into convulsions. Gas uncontrollably came out of his butt, but he was alive. Stinking greasy, black, and ugly, but alive! I must be alive, too! Joey looked at me and asked if I was okay. I tried to stand up on limber legs that betrayed me. "Thanks," I uttered in embarrassment and shame.

In Pankey Town we played in the mudhole almost every day. Well, we often splashed and stuck our heads down to our feet. This was Cape Hatteras, and it had a well-earned historical reputation as the "Graveyard of the Atlantic."

We went to see "The Lost Colony." I didn't talk or eat. The Indians and Pilgrims seemed real. The bow and arrows were impressive to a 16 year old from the cotton and tobacco fields of Laurinburg, North Carolina. I learned a very powerful lesson. "You don't drown if you fall in the water. You drown if you don't get out."

Embarrassment was my silent companion for the rest of my summer at NCSA. Joey was the muscle-bound girl whom other students called "Butch" behind her back. Before my summer at the school, I had never heard of gay, lesbian, butch or homosexual. These were new terms to me. Same sex relationships were never discussed in Pankey Town. I was learning new stuff and new prejudices. A white girl had saved my life. Racism was part of the southern culture. This girl was a total stranger to me. What about my readings about the Black Panther Party, Bobby Seals, Huey P, Newton, Malcolm, The Nation of Islam and Marcus Garvey? You can't rewrite your history, can you? Race, gender, religion and sexual orientation took a back seat to a born again experience that challenged many "country fool" beliefs. They, not me, drowned in the waters of Manteo, North Carolina. Let the dead bury the dead!

Riots & School Integration

Upon my return to Scotland High School, Ms. Narromore, my drama teacher and the person responsible for my summer experience at the N.C. School of The Arts, asked about my experience. My embellished story focused on drama, music, dance and speech classes. My near-death experience was never discussed. Who would understand?

Scotland High School was integrated around 1967. The change brought with it deep-rooted resentment, fear and hate. Violence, race riots and brutal fights were new to the students at the newly constructed comprehensive high school. Small incidents would blow up into big fights without any warnings. The student commons and school cafeteria often erupted like a racial neutron bomb. It was impossible to separate the good guys from the bad guys. It happened! You would get hit and you closed your eyes and swing back. If a friend fought, you fought, too. There were very few rules except you fought to defend anybody that looked like you. There was an unwritten rule that you tried to stay out of stuff, but we were all trapped in a history of racism and bigotry that had met its predestination.

Martin Luther King, Jr. was killed April 4, 1968. Black students cried, but some of our white classmates laughed. They waved confederate flags at us. We gathered around the American flag that was now lowered at half-mast. Rednecks raised the flag back up and defiantly said that Dr. King deserved to die. All hell broke loose. Students picked up bricks, broken bottles, chairs and anything else they could get their hands on. None of us was immune to friends involved in shouting racial epithets, throwing objects, punching, kicking, biting, overturning cars, breaking glass, and chronic suspensions. Hate, raw emotions, fear and uncertainty became the core curriculum.

Jimmy Webb, a white classmate, and I were appointed co-chairmen of the Human Relations Council. We often met and discussed ways to improve interracial conflicts. We sincerely tried our best. The conflicts never fully subsided, but we graduated in June 1970 without major incidents. Racial

6

fights were not considered major incidents. They were part of growing up in Southern hospitality. I graduated in 1970. The excellent leadership of Principal Doug Yongue guided the school through a very difficult period of racial strife. The Laurinburg Human Betterment Committee gave me an award for the person most exemplifying the teachings of Jesus Christ. But nothing prepared me for the next four years.

North Carolina School Of The Arts Years

World-class filmmakers, set designers, visual and performing artists, temper tantrums, auditions, hours of rehearsals, geniuses, masterpieces, cross-dressing, drugs and sexual promiscuity were some of the (worst-kept) secrets at the North Carolina School Of The Arts. My undergraduate years from 1970-74 shattered whatever innocence I had left after experiencing the deaths of John F. Kennedy, Martin Luther King Jr., Robert Kennedy, and Malcolm X.

NCSA was a pendulum between a torture chamber and jubilation.

The school's curriculum and staff are some of the best in the world. The speech classes were the most embarrassing. I had speech tutorials for 4 years. My speech was terrible. Although I won the NCSA Karate Championship, produced a play, and received the Nancy Reynolds Merit Award in drama, learning to speak Standard English was a seemingly insurmountable task. Someone said I talked like I had marbles in my mouth. This was not unusual for a small town country boy, but it was devastating for a drama major at the North Carolina School of the Arts.

Many nights I would lay awake, recalling my childhood of a one-room house, leaking roof, outdoor toilets, toiling in the noon sun, fed broken English, and surrounded by uneducated relatives. I came to realize the mountain I attempted to climb was slippery and littered with broken glass.

Many Black students were failing at NCSA and leaving before Thanksgiving. There were times when I cried myself to sleep, drunk with self-pity. Big nosed, big lipped, slurred speech, skin bronzed, blacker than most Africans' skin, glittering like a 50 cent shoeshine, I felt like a demoralized Colored, Negro, Black African American fool trying to perform Shakespeare and felt like a total country idiot. My second year, I attended NCSA's drama program at Stockwell College in Bromley, Kent, England. I thought world-renowned actor Sir Lawrence Olivier was Mr. Oliver.

Yet the NC School of The Arts was an extraordinary training institution for aspiring artists. One of our favorite drama teachers, William Jaeger, impressed many Black students. He became our loud and opinionated Jewish advocate. I played Bobby in his production of Ceremonies in Dark Old Men. Later, we demanded Black courses and an annual Black Arts Festival. The North Carolina School of The Arts was located on Waughtown Street in Winston Salem, North Carolina. It had a total of 500 students. Fifty of us were Black.

However, I never would have survived without the support of my cousin, David Pankey, Jr. David was always there for me when I needed him. He introduced me to Think and Grow Rich, written by Napoleon Hill. Hill's philosophy of organized planning and a positive mental attitude would become my main ally for challenges and adversity waiting for me later in life.

One would think that leaving home and going to college would erase memories and problems would be left behind. Pankey Town is part of my history. It is who I am. I was sheltered, naive and innocent. I had no idea what was in store for me in college. However, N. C. School Of The Arts afforded me an opportunity to reflect on my spiritual beliefs and seek an identity. Lesley Hunt, my speech teacher and tutor, worked with me on speaking correct standard American speech. Lesley was a saint. Despite stubbornness and resistance, her words finally pierced through my defensive layers of resentment, fear, insecurity and anxiety. "If you want to speak like Martin Luther King, you must learn to speak well. The objective is to be a universal actor. You must be clearly understood by everyone." Bob and Mollie Murray, as well as Guyla Pandi, instilled in me a love for drama and dance that accelerated my development as a performer. It took years of practice, but I did a monologue of King Lear as the drama representative at the NCSA senior recital.

My life of poverty and fear of staying poor built a shield that frightened me away from free drugs and kegs of beer available at NCSA. Every adult in Pankey Town contributed to disciplining and raising each child. Pankey Town taught me very good core values. These values were often tested.

One of my closest friends in college was karate black belt David Jonathan Tillman from Buffalo, New York. He had me purchase books by Matsutatso Oyama. Oyama was a legendary karate teacher or sensei. (I still own my original books.) Dave was my karate teacher. He would wake me up at 5:00 a.m. each day for rigorous training in the old school way that did not include mats or pads. Dave could play over ten musical instruments and played the piano as if he invented it. He was a great teacher and many students benefited from his exposing us to the teachings of Eastern religion, meditation and karate.

My idolization of him was temporarily shattered when he was involved in an off campus drug bust. Most geniuses fight with demons and devils, as well as a dark side. My karate sensei and hero was allegedly the campus pusher. I knew the truth, but neither the police nor school officials ever bothered to ask me. My father's problems with alcohol instilled in me a sense of fear about drugs and alcohol. I never had an interest in drugs and simply looked away. Yet my level of dependence and search for a strong black male figure led me back to Dave. Dave taught me karate for free. He never offered me drugs. He often stated that he wished he had my level of restraint and discipline. I admired his karate ability. Dave practiced karate at least two hours a day. He also spent one or more hours practicing the piano, and his major instrument, the bassoon. His talent was awesome. He was the school's Black version of Bruce Lee. He and I went to see Bruce Lee movies over and over again. As a result of his training, I won the NCSA Karate Championship in 1973. A few years later, my letters to Dave kept coming back. He had been killed in a car accident. Bruce Lee had died earlier. Both my karate heroes were now dead. Dave Tillman and Bruce Lee played different, but very significant roles in my life.

The NCSA experience was punctuated with never ending classical vs. contemporary artistic verbal debates. The gays and butches constantly engaged in bitch sessions about their claim to "Divahood." Heterosexuals struggled for peaceful coexistence with a very talented, but highly emotional gay population.

For the first time in my life, I experienced discrimination as a heterosexual. (Seriously, I did not even know the meaning of gay or lesbian until my summer school experience at NCSA.) Sex, birth control, condoms and abortions became a regular part of cafeteria conversations. I pretended to be in the know. Hell, in high school, sex was a rare accomplishment. Like a lot of other guys, I kept a rubber in my wallet until it left a permanent imprint on the leather. Dancing the "slow drag" while listening to the Dells' hit song, Stay in My Corner, was as close to sex as a lot of kids in my high school experienced. However, sex was a normal part of college life. Nobody made a big deal about it. However, there was often a conflict between meaningful significant others and recreation. Break-ups were plentiful, painful and melodramatic.

Arguments, suspicions, and accusations were intense. Black students struggled with Eurocentric, Afrocentric, and the classical perception of art and beauty. Who's the Blackest? Who's Afro American? Were we Afro or African American? Who's an Uncle Tom? This was the era of Vietnam, protests, Eugene McCarthy, George McGovern, Barry Goldwater, Kent State University, the Black Panthers, hippies, drugs, sex, and rock and roll. We questioned all views, authority figures, and political persuasions.

Trust no one over 30.

NCSA Superstars

Several of my NCSA classmates became superstars. Belinda Tolbert emerged as our idol because of her recurring role as Jeannie on the Jeffersons. Paulette Pearson graduated and eventually married Academy Award winner Denzel Washington. She was one of the school's most versatile and talented singer-pianists. Glenda Wharton's art as a painter and film animation artist has received well deserved accolades. Joe Henderson became a highly respected Shakespearean scholar. Cynthia Penn-Henderson joined the Alvin Ailey dance company and received rave reviews. Thomas Hulce received an academy award nomination for Amadeus. Terrence Mann starred on Broadway in Les Miserables. Glyn O'Malley became an award-winning playwright. Gwendolyn Bradely became a household name in artistic circles as she gave them fever at the Metropolitan Opera. Marilyn McIntyre became a soap opera star. Joyce Rheeling became a television commercial queen. Ron Dortch and Steve Henderson went to Broadway. The NC School of the Arts has graduates either on stage or behind the set for major shows on Broadway, television and movies. Approximately 90% of the school's design and production majors have landed jobs. The success of graduates have earned the school well deserved international acclaim for its movie stars, playwrights, directors dancers, musicians, composers, and costume designers. The North Carolina School of the Arts is a national treasure.

The University Of Maryland Years

After graduation from NCSA, I went to graduate school at the University of Maryland. The Drama Department's staff was all white. Only two Black students were in the graduate program. I was given many white roles, but I pleaded for an opportunity to play Black characters. I was ignored. Most of the professors were relatively supportive, but Professor O'Leary proved to be inflexible. He was assigned as my graduate thesis adviser. I rebelled. I quit for two weeks. I was in search of my Black identity. Despite 4 years of classical training at NCSA, I knew I would be pegged as a Black artist. I wanted to do Black theatre. I had already done Othello, King Lear, Julius Caesar, and The Glass Menagerie. I considered leaving and moving to New York City. My cousin Jerome convinced me to stay. Jerome was adamant that Pankeys do not quit. He reiterated, "You can't quit every time things do not go your way."

Despite mild controversy and a few temper tantrums, Professor Roger Meersman guided me through research on Black theatre. I received my MA Degree in Speech-Theatre. Dr. Meersman was a good mentor. Jerome made it clear that many horses start races, but only thoroughbreds finish. I would not have completed grad school without Dr. Meersman and Jerome. I continued writing plays, did Othello, Peer Gynt and developed a one-man show impersonating Dick Gregory at Kent State. I worked on several comedy routines and impersonations.

Eyes On Broadway

Right before graduation from the University Of Maryland, I received a small speaking part in the movie The Brotherhood of Death with Washington Redskins stars Roy Jefferson and Mike Thomas. After graduation, I moved to New York City. I wanted to work as a professional actor, comedian and impressionist. Unable to find steady work, I worked as a typist. My work as an office temp gave me invaluable insights into the workings of at least 50 major corporations. Unemployment gave me a lot of free time to audition, mail out photos, develop a one-man show and read hours at a time. Reading, writing, and brooding became routine until I began substitute teaching for the New York City Board of Education.

Agents often complimented me for my auditions, but called me for only one industrial film. I was disheartened by my experience with casting agents. They consistently told me to change my look, get new photographs, and get agency representation. Once, I waited two hours to see a receptionist. I had a seemingly good conversation and left my photo/resume with her. I left her office but immediately returned to ask her another question. My photo/resume was in the garbage can by her desk. Working as a teacher gave me a dependable paycheck. I had gone weary of eviction notices.

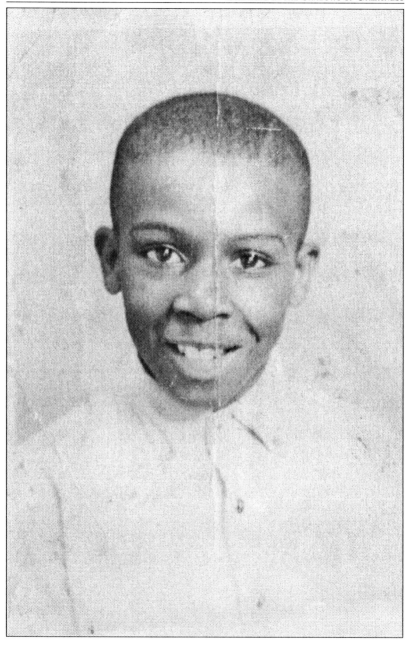

Henry Pankey at age 10.

Childhood homes. (Above) Brother James A. Pankey standing in barn converted into a bedroom and kitchen, 1952-1959; (left) new house in 1959 complete with electricity, running water and indoor toilet installed in 1973.

Victorian style 12-room house in Flatbush section of Brooklyn, NY, 1981-1996.

Hot summer day in Pankey Town. Jesse Pankey, Edgar Harrington and James Pankey.

(Top left) The Matriarch of the family, Ms. Mamie McDuffie Pankey, often worked double shifts at Scotland Memorial Hospital for 32 years. She sent four of her six children to college. (Above) Proud parents Mamie and Jessie Pankey, 1992.

Sunday after church. Henry Pankey, James Pankey, Ms. Mamie Pankey and David Owens, 1980.

Mamie Pankey celebrates her son's first national publicity, Blac*Tress Magazine, 1979.

Steve Henderson, Henry Pankey, and David Parker, Ceremonies In Dark Old Men, directed by William Jaeger, 1971.

North Carolina School
of the Arts, 1972.

The Madonna and Child.
Henry Pankey and Ms.
Ruby Wharton, 1973.

Henry Pankey,
actor, comedian,
impressionist,
publicity photo,
1978.

Henry Pankey and
Nancy Mette stage
fighting at Stockwell
College, Bromley,
Kent, England, 1972.

17

Henry Pankey with his wife, Aleyah and their three children, Ashia, Amira and Aaron.

Father and son, 2002.

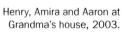

Henry, Amira and Aaron at Grandma's house, 2003.

Ashia and Aleyah celebrate Ashia's graduation from Jordan High School, 2003.

Amira Pankey is crowned Miss 1999 Honeydoll at North Carolina Central University.

19

(Above) Pankey at Hillside High School, 2002. (Right) Breaking with tradition by declaring Dr. Susan S. McKinney JHS 265 a "prep school." Zero tolerance for misbehavior, dress for success, unconditional commitment to excellence, no excuses, and prep for success academic initiatives, 1992. Ed Corbett photo.

Scotland High School's Assistant Principal Bill Parker looks on as Pankey patrols the halls as Batman, 1996.

Dressed as a "Fighting Scot," Scotland High School, 1997.

Henry, Amira, Ashia and Aleyah in Scotland County's 1996 Christmas Parade. Superintendent Dr. John Batchelor and Assistant Superintendent Norwood Randolph follow in second car.

21

Making History. Scotland High School's first African American principal, 1996.

Pankey Town's first college graduate, Pauline McDuffie, graduated from Fayetteville State University in 1960.

Students loved "Dress for Success" at Dr. Susan McKinney, JHS 265. From diamonds in the rough to crown jewels in the 17th largest project in the country, 1993.

Scotland High School students receive "Dress for Success" awards and incentives, 1996.

The New York City Council of Administrators presented the Effective School Award to Dr. Susan S. McKinney JHS 265 at the CSA Leadership Conference on December 3, 1994. (from left: Ed Corbett, coordinator; Henry Pankey, principal; Donald Singer, president of CSA; Helen Henderson, coordinatior; Dennis Hinson, assistant principal)

"We must love all students unconditionally."
Carrington Middle School, 2003.

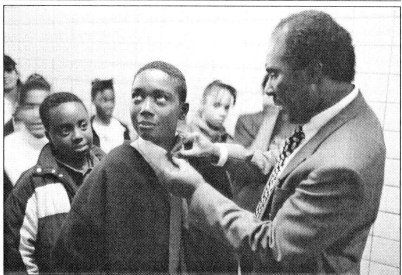

How to tie a necktie? JHS 265 students look on as Principal Pankey demon-strates, 1992. Jon Naso photograph.

Hillside High School senior Shannon Moore joins the principal on hall patrol, 2002.

Principal Pankey shows JHS 265 students "Ole School" dance steps.
Halloween, 1992. Jon Naso photograph.

MAN WITH THE PLAN

The Herald-Sun/PETER SCHUMACHER

Southern High School students get moving when Principal Henry Pankey walks the hall between classes. Always on the lookout for dress-code infractions, he believes neat students do better in school.

'No-nonsense' principal turns Southern High around

By ROBIN L. REALE
The Herald-Sun

"Who's that?"

Henry Pankey, Southern High School's new principal, barked the question as he pointed with his walkie-talkie to one of dozens of students fresh off the bus and on their way to class.

The boy who caught his attention stopped in his tracks and, looking nervous, plodded over to Pankey.

"Are you on the football team?"

The boy nodded slowly, shifting his eyes to see his friends go on without him.

"Thanks for dressing up," Pankey said, checking out the dress shirt and tie. He patted the student's back and sent him, visibly relieved, on his way.

It's the same every morning — Pankey standing in the front lobby, greeting students, making sure they have notebooks and inspecting their clothing.

Shirts must be tucked in. Shoes must be tied. Belts must be worn with skirts or pants, and pants must be worn above the waist.

One student started shoving the back of his red shirt into his knee-length blue shorts as he passed Pankey.

"You've got to do a little bit better, man, but you're halfway there," Pankey said.

Teachers, parents and even

The Herald-Sun/PETER SCHUMACHER

STRAIGHT AND NARROW: Southern High School Principal Henry Pankey straightens the tie of ninth-grader Doug Tsao as Doug arrived at school recently. Pankey was poking fun at his strait-laced image.

many students applaud Pankey's strict enforcement of rules Southern didn't have last year.

After only two weeks this year, they say, morale no longer is low, there is mutual respect in the classroom and, for the first time in a while, education is taking priority over discipline problems.

Everyone seems confident Southern, as a result of the changes, will post higher-than-usual test scores on this year's standardized exams.

Superintendent Ann Denlinger already has pledged to make sure of that. Just under 36 percent of

please see **SOUTHERN**/A2

'No-Nonsense' principal turns Southern High around, headline, Herald Sun, Durham, North Carolina, August 31, 1998.

26

EDITORIALS

SOUTHERN HIGH SCHOOL

Durham Herald Sun,
January 26, 1999.

The Pankey way

Southern High School Principal Henry Pankey's no-nonsense style has earned him as many enemies as friends. Even some Southern parents, as was apparent from some letters to The Herald-Sun's Editorial page, were put off by the buttoned-down disciplinarian who refused to overlook even the slightest infractions.

But after six months of doing it the Pankey way, many of his critics are starting to come around. In fact, you can count on many of Pankey's critics to sing his praises — and with good reason. After years of languishing in the Durham Public Schools' academic cellar, Southern is on the rise and moving toward respectability.

This academic year, Southern just might shed the low-performing status it earned from the N.C. Department of Public Instruction last spring when very few — less than 36 percent — of its students tested at or above grade level.

Word of Southern's remarkable transformation isn't just hearsay or wishful thinking. The evidence can be found in first semester test scores, where gains were made in nearly every discipline. In English 2, for example, 52.6 percent of students performed at grade level or better the first semester — an astounding 34.8 percent improvement over the 17.8 percent who did so in the 1997-98 academic year.

In fact, the only subject where Southern lost ground was in physics, where the percentage of students who performed at or above grade level slipped a modest 4.3 percent.

Pankey supporters credit Southern's phenomenal turnaround to the principal's strict enforcement of the rules. Students must obey the school's dress code — male and female students alike must keep shirt tails tucked. And more importantly, Pankey demands that students treat teachers and each other with respect. As a result, teachers say they are spending less time maintaining order in the classroom these days.

Pankey is an admirable throwback to the good old days when principals were in full control the schools in their care. And Southern High is a prime example of what can be accomplished when schools are run the Pankey way.

The Herald-Sun
DAVID HUGHEY
Publisher and president
JON C. HAM
Managing editor
WILLIAM E.N. HAWKINS
Vice president and executive editor
JAMES R. WILSON
Editorial page editor
TUESDAY, JANUARY 26, 1999

Raleigh News & Observer,
January 24, 1999.

Tough classes pay off

It's perhaps too easy to lionize Principal Henry Pankey for the dramatic improvement in state test scores at the school he leads, Durham's Southern High. But then, Pankey deserves much of the praise. The no-nonsense principal came to Southern last year shortly after it was declared Durham's only "low-performing" high school under the state's school improvement plan. He has insisted on a good learning climate and high standards.

Pankey's attitude is increasingly popular in the United States, and it's welcome. Simply put, educators are setting respectable standards and expecting the best from students academically. All over the country, school systems are making greater demands on 12th graders before granting diplomas. In his State of the Union speech last week, President Clinton called for an end to social promotions. North Carolina recently moved to do that. The call for higher standards is filtering down to the teachers' ranks. Several states, including North Carolina, have made teacher education and licensing more rigorous.

The value of all this, of course, is that schools will turn out better-educated students. It also promises to strengthen trust in the public schools. They have been justly criticized for expecting too little of students, in academics and behavior. Tough new schoolmasters such as Pankey prove that American children can in fact consistently rise to the task of learning.

THE NEWS & OBSERVER
SUNDAY, JANUARY 24, 1999

National Alliance Of Black School Educators 1999 Hall of Fame Recipient of the Ida B. Wells Hall Of Fame Award, November 12, 1999.

The News & Observer
Friday, June 11, 1999

Editorial

The principal principle

The News
& Observer,
Raleigh,
North Carolina,
June 11, 1999.

Tough-talking, no-nonsense Henry Pankey, principal of Durham's Southern High School, is every ill-behaved, unmotivated student's nightmare. But Pankey is every parent's dream in this unsettled age of schoolhouse massacres, failing discipline and anemic academic achievement.

Pankey has shown that tough but thoughtful school standards can be progressive and compassionate. After a few decades' fling with squishy discipline and "relative" academic measurements, school administrators are returning to common-sense expectations of good behavior and real academic effort. Those virtues are paying off at Southern High.

It's obvious that the problem at Southern wasn't necessarily the students. In one year of Pankey's leadership, Southern has gone from a place of chaos in many ways — rife with fights, racial tension and low academic achievement — to orderly hallways and end-of-course test scores that surged ahead in 10 of 11 categories. Pankey requires students to dress neatly and appropriately, a far-from-brutal demand that other troubled Triangle schools could copy.

One suspects that students are better able to learn because they feel more secure. Pankey has increased security measures at Southern, and students must have a pass if venturing outside the classroom, a once common but often neglected measure today. Teachers' morale has soared. It's likely that they are able to concentrate on practicing their vocations rather than their survival skills. A mark of Pankey's concern for learning — rather than just discipline — is a scholarship fund he has started for Southern High graduates.

Solid elementary schools help set the course of children's lives, while effective middle and high schools launch academic or vocational careers. And a school's ability to put its students on the right track depends greatly on the skills of its principal. In Henry Pankey, the students of Southern High, and their community, now have a classic example of how much influence a good principal can have.

Friday, January 7, 2000

Editorial: Metaphor for success

The News
& Observer
Online,
Raleigh,
North
Carolina,
January 7,
2000.

Here's an intriguing topic for an English paper: Southern High School as a metaphor for the significant advances in education in North Carolina. Give Richard Riley, the U.S. secretary of education, an A because that's why he picked the once-troubled school in Durham County, in a state that is making steady strides in education, as the backdrop for his seventh annual State of American Education address.

Governor Hunt's attention to educational attainment has made the state a fitting showplace. Students in North Carolina have begun the slow climb out of the basement of national achievement test scores. As Riley noted in announcing Southern High as the site of his Feb. 22 address, Hunt has championed better teacher training and pay. His emphasis on early childhood education is feeding better-prepared students into the public schools. He also has been an effective advocate for safe schools and more technology in the classroom.

Hunt's reputation as a pioneer in education reform is known nationally (Riley, of course, was a fellow reform leader while serving as governor of South Carolina). Southern High is better known locally, but formerly for the wrong reasons: a dismal record of achievement and a reputation for violence. But a change of principals has transformed Southern into a high-achieving, orderly place.

In large measure, North Carolina (and Southern High) languished educationally because of a lack of vision and leadership. Hunt and *Henry Pankey*, the principal and architect of the astounding improvements at Southern, have provided the needed ingredients.

At Southern, Riley is scheduled to talk about the progress made since his first State of American Education speech in 1994. He picked an excellent place.

29

U.S. secretary of education to speak at Southern High

By DEREK HUTCHINS
Under Construction crew

The hard work during the past couple of years at Southern High School has paid off with a visit from the U.S. secretary of education slated later this month.

Richard Riley will deliver his seventh State of American Education Address from Southern High's gym at noon on Feb. 22. During the annual address, Riley will discuss the improvements that have been made in the education system since his first address in 1994.

"[Riley's] selection of Southern High School as the site from which to address the nation ... reflects not only on the success of our teachers and students, but indeed on the significant gains realized by our school system and the state of North Carolina," Southern Principal Henry Pankey said.

Southern was chosen for the address due to the jump in its performance status. Southern made the largest gains, struggling from being the lowest performing school in the district, to achieving exemplary status just one year later.

Guidance counselor Linda Carmichael said that students and faculty are honored.

"Out of all the schools, we got picked. This is an extraordinary event to happen at Southern High School," she said.

Some Southern students were unexcited about Riley coming, however.

"We'd rather have a baseball player come," said senior Tessa Baker and freshman Justin Jenkins.

In previous years, Riley has given the annual address at California State University, Long Beach; Nathan Eckstein Middle School in Seattle; the Carter Center in Atlanta with former President Jimmy Carter; Maplewood-Richmond Heights Senior High School in St. Louis; Thomas Jefferson Middle School in Arlington, Va.; and Georgetown University in Washington, D.C.

U.S. Secretary of Education Richard Riley (left) will deliver his seventh State of American Education address from Southern High's gym at noon on Feb. 22. Southern Principal Henry Pankey (above) says the visit reflects on the school's recent success.

ASSOCIATED PRESS

The Durham Herald Sun, February, 2000.

30

Top photo: U.S. Secretary of Education Richard Riley (right) accepts a gift from Southern High School student body president Sandy Strickland following Riley's seventh annual State of American Education speech on Tuesday at the Durham school.
Left photo: Southern principal Henry Pankey (center) sits with his daughter Amira, 7, between Durham mayor Nick Tennyson (left) and U.S. Rep. Mike McIntyre, D-N.C., as they listen to Riley's speech at Southern.

TOP PHOTO: THE HERALD-SUN/JOE WEISS
LEFT PHOTO: THE HERALD-SUN/KEVIN SEIFERT

United Education Secretary Richard Riley visits Southern High School, February 23, 2000. Durham Herald Sun.

U. S. SECRETARY OF EDUCATION
RICHARD W. RILEY
CORDIALLY INVITES YOU TO ATTEND

THE SEVENTH ANNUAL
STATE OF AMERICAN EDUCATION ADDRESS

TUESDAY, FEBRUARY 22, 2000
TWELVE O'CLOCK NOON
(EASTERN STANDARD TIME)

SOUTHERN HIGH SCHOOL
800 CLAYTON ROAD
DURHAM, NORTH CAROLINA

From the cotton fields of North Carolina
to the national stage, 2000.

Riley greets Henry Pankey, the principal
of Southern High School in Durham. (AP
Photo)

United States Secretary Richard Riley delivered the Seventh Annual State of American
Education Address from Southern High School, February 22, 2000.

Hillside's new dance craze

You keep The Good Kids IN!
You kick The Bad kids out! ♪
You stress some Dis-Ci-Pline
And use a Bullhorn ♪
♪ When you shout!!
You Do The Hanky-Pankey
And you turn The School Around!
And That's What
♪ It's All About!! ♪

Published June 1, 2001
E-mail John Cole at crj@herald-sun.com

A BULLHORN, A DRESS CODE AND SOME OLD-FASHIONED SELF-RESPECT

In the stairs with his bullhorn, the new principal of Southern High, Henry Pankey, encourages students to get on their way without loitering. His theory — that good discipline is a precondition to learning— is not radical, but some of his methods are.
STAFF PHOTO BY CHUCK LIDDY

Sending his message loud and clear

A former actor seizes the spotlight as a principal trying to transform a troubled Durham high school

BY MICHELE KURTZ
STAFF WRITER

DURHAM — On patrol at Southern High School, Principal Henry Pankey growls through a bullhorn at a student whose sloppy dress offends his sensibilities.

"You're busted, man."

At Southern, a new set of rules is on the books: Tuck in your shirt and wear a belt. Carry a notebook to school every day. And get ready to walk through a metal detector.

The rules address the obvious, but they're part of a deeper cure prescribed by Pankey, a former New York City principal and former actor brought to Durham this fall to transform the school — the only one in the Triangle to be slapped with a low-performing label this year by the state.

Situated in the east end of Durham County, Southern long has labored in the shadow of Durham's other high schools, like Jordan, which consistently has the best test scores in the county.

In the past few years, though, Southern's struggle has become more acute. Two principals have left. Its enrollment has dropped by 200 students — mostly in the past year. By most accounts, the student body had become increasingly unruly, with many students roaming the halls and refusing to go to class. Teachers said they found themselves spending more time addressing behavior problems and less on academics.

And this year, Southern got the state's lowest ranking because only 36 percent of students tested in core courses performed at grade level last spring.

"We have been very concerned with the situation at Southern," says Kathy Carpenter, a parent and herself a graduate of the school. "So many of the students had disrespect for themselves as well as authority."

Pankey, 46, says all that is going to change — fast. And when discipline improves, he says, so will learning.

With a mixture of "psyched-up

SEE **PANKEY**, PAGE 10A

Raleigh News & Observer, September 27, 1998.

33

The long walk...
Last day at Hillside High School, 2002.

Nature's Way Of Training A Leader, God Or King

Because we don't understand the incomprehensible ways of Mother Nature, we are quick to call her cruel. Nature's training techniques are ultimately kind. Angela Morgan's poem is a remarkable testimonial of the mysterious, but wonderful ways Nature prepares a future leader for his destiny:

> When Nature wants to take a man,
> And shake a man,
> And wake a man;
> When Nature wants to make a man
> To do the Future's will;
> When she yearns with all her soul
> To create him large and whole...
> With what cunning she prepares him,
> How she goads and never spares him!
> How she whets him, and she frets him,
> And in poverty begets him...
> How she often disappoints
> Whom she sacredly anoints,
> With what wisdom she will hide him,
> Never minding what betide him
> Though his genius sob with slighting and his
> Pride may not forget!
> Bids him struggle harder yet...
>
> When Nature wants to name a man
> And fame a man
> And tame a man;
> When Nature wants to shame a man
> To do his heavenly best...
> When she tries the highest test
> That she reckoning may bring
> When she wants a god or king!

How she reins him and restrains him
So his body scarce contains him
While she fires him
And inspires him!
Keeps him yearning, ever burning
for a tantalizing goal
Lures and lacerates his soul….

Nature's plan is wondrous kind
Could we understand her mind…
Fools are they who call her blind.
When his feet are torn and bleeding
Yet his spirit mounts unheeding,
All his higher powers speeding,
Blazing newer paths and fine;
When the force that is divine
Leaps to challenge every failure
and his ardor still is sweet
And love and hope are burning
in the presence of defeat…
Lo, the crisis! Lo, the shout
That must call the leader out.
When the people need salvation
Doth he come to lead the nation…
Then doth Nature show her plan
When the world has found a MAN!

It would be a tragic misrepresentation to conclude my childhood was only land-mined with poverty, misery, disrepair and self-hatred. The antithesis of being raised like a junkyard dog or rented mule was pride, faith, love, and hope. They contributed to memorable experiences that embedded a permanent respect of work, education, respect, and an affinity for meticulous dress.

Primal years in the one-room shack during my childhood in Pankey Town were often the source of ridicule for five children struggling to endure freezing winters and the merciless wind blowing through the cracks of the red barn called home for the first six years of my life. My family slept on the floor on blankets we called pallets. Hell, you could see and count the chickens walking under the house/barn. We cuddled to keep warm and prayed no one peed in their sleep. We were often unlucky. Many nights someone peed in the bed. We shared washrags and toothbrushes. We can't deny the past.

In 1959 the family moved into a 3-bedroom blockhouse that was built by my daddy and uncles. Ma bought all the supplies and paid for the mortgage without any money from Daddy. A few years later we got electricity, but kept kerosene lamps in case daddy went into one of his drunken rages and hid the fuses or didn't pay the light bill prior to the mandatory shut offs. Like other Southern men, he beat his wife and kids. We may deny it today, but Southern men used to beat the living hell out of their wives, children, each other, and farm animals. The South has a "hush hush" history of violence that included immunity from prosecution. Watching my father beat my mother and physically abuse us was a fear that temporarily subsided when he was asleep, at work, in jail for the weekend, or on the chain gang. Once, Ma got tired of the beatings and threw fish grease on him. He ran out of the house, screaming like a pig in mid-slaughter. Grandma cut off his shirt. Skin stayed on his t-shirt. His meat came off like a piece of red bacon – pinkish warped skin that turned watermelon red. When he came from the hospital, Ma applied salve and removed wrappings from a permanently disfigured back.

Unfortunately, the fights, stealing money, cutting up clothes, destroying furniture, shooting, and burning parts of the house became routines. Most of us maintained passing grades despite having to read or study in the dark. Women at the bootlegger houses took his money. He failed to pay the light bill, hid fuses or denied us permission to use kerosene lamps or candles. We didn't know if he was crazy, an alcoholic or just hated us. We knew no other life. Other kids had mean daddies, too. We pretend none of this stuff has ever happened. Time is cruel and will not bring closure. We forgive. We will never understand. We will never forget.

My brother James and I often discussed ways to find a permanent solution, but we couldn't come up with a plan. We didn't want to go to jail. We loved our daddy, but we were afraid of him. We just wanted the pain to stop. We wanted to eat and sleep in peace. We wanted food, clothing, shelter, love, and Christmas like some, but not all, of our friends. My three sisters, James and I chronically begged Ma to file court papers for non-support. We got tired and embarrassed of asking cousins for their old biscuits, ham, etc. Each of us became creative cooking hotcakes. Syrup, bacon, ham and eggs were luxury items we knew we'd have at least the first week my mother received her monthly check from working at Scotland Memorial Hospital as a nurse's aid. When daddy went on the chain gang for non-support, the welfare gave us yellow grits, non-rising flour, canned meat, high top shoes, money, and a monthly dose of shame.

My mother and daddy's side of the family consistently offered support and words of encouragement. A few on Daddy's side were mean, condescending and critical of our life of poverty. However, others were lovingly and deeply concerned about our well-being. We were often the blunt jokes, laughed at because of our dark skin, nappy heads and drunken father. Like other Blacks, we used bleaching cream and hair straighteners. Blacks made fun of their "Negro" features and dark skin during the 50's and 60's. Some of our relatives did not invite us to dinner or parties. We sometimes saw them eating "high on the hog," but we knew not to cross the property line. We felt cemented at the bottom of the family's caste system. Still, we were all proud to be Pankeys. Ma taught us to be proud. She bragged that we made the honor roll. We were smart in school.

Grandpa Luther Frank McDuffie gave his grandchildren rides in his car and gave us candy and sodas. He was a fearless speaker with a thunderous voice and eyes the size of quarters. He constantly told me I was the "one". He said I'd grow up to be a preacher. Grandpa was a dark-skinned, tall, lanky, charismatic man who took center stage in any room he entered. When Grandpa would preach, the windows in the church would shake, rattle and roll. Grandpa was all-powerful, but the amputation of his legs frightened and confused me.

Ironically, while other kids were breaking into homes and stores, my cousin David and I would break into the church for our prayer meetings. David would play the piano for hours and I'd preach until my strained throat became hoarse and voiceless. My first cousin Jerome was the deacon and bishop of the amen corner. I danced across the pulpit and preached the gospel to the "chillun" of Pankey Town! God, I loved to open up the Bible and put on a show. I could imitate most preachers. I'd preach, pray, sweat, wave my handkerchief, do the Jackie Wilson split, dance, and cry. Something got a hold of me. It was either the Lord or the Devil. We'd invite our cousins to prayer meetings. They paid us with pennies. Grandma Ada Pankey said we were playing with God. Much later in my life, I did the sermon routine for my successful audition into the N. C. School of the Arts undergraduate drama program.

When I was about five years old, I begged my parents for the self-esteem-building cotton picking assignment and was later promoted to the tobacco field. Ted Harrington and Beulah Monley were neighborhood stars because they could pick over 200 pounds of cotton a day. Many of us cheated by watering cotton, adding dirt, stalks, and foreign objects to our day's harvest, but few topped 200 pounds. My grandmother out-picked me. I never picked more than 150 pounds. My other heroes were my cousins, Eddie Frank, Pappy, Bill, Geneboy, and my brother James. They could outwork anybody.

As guys in Pankey Town got older, they were allowed to stay at the tobacco farm or given the much-cherished assignment of cropping tobacco. We spent our money on school clothes, but had to give most of it to Daddy. Usually I bought 2 shirts, and 2 pairs of pants for school.

Eventually, field heroes were replaced by Pauline McDuffie. She was the first person in Pankey Town to finish college. Pankey Town's Allen Chapel AME Church rituals were a major contribution to my spiritual awakening and establishment of a vehement belief in God. Religious folks confused and confounded my sense of sinners and saints. The neighborhood drunks and gossipers were the deacons, preachers, choir members, ushers and saints on Sunday. Church was the haven for gossipers. Most people in Pankey Town were hard workers and expressed their belief in God. A few parishioners smelled of old liquor, chewing gum, mouthwash and cheap cologne. However, my mother always taught us to wear clean clothes everyday, especially on Sunday. Cleanliness was next to Godliness. Little did I know that her lessons of dressing in our Sunday's best would have implications for a national Dress for Success program thirty years later. This basic training taught me that you reap what you sow. On the farm, what you plant and nurture is what comes up. "God is still in charge" was our daily prayer.

My sisters Pat, Betty, and Jessie Lee taught me to read and write before I entered the first grade. Later in my career, literacy would become a formidable challenge that I would face as a principal. My sisters insisted that I behave, have discipline and learn to "dramatize" poetry. I was the class clown. I would finish my work ahead of everybody else and clown. I was bored and could not sit for long periods of time. Although I received over ten disciplinary whippings a week in elementary school, the ongoing corporal punishment never interfered with my reputation as a smart boy. In the sixth grade I tutored boys who had flunked. They were older and bigger, but were protective of their younger bookworm. The lessons of improving literacy, discipline, patience, tutoring others, and respect for slow students would be major principles of a principal decades later. (As a highly paid national school consultant, how could I tell educators that most of what I learned about reading was taught to me by my sisters?) Reviewing the past unveils a hidden secret that seems to confirm that a universal force shapes our lives and molds us for the future. Working in the fields and on the farm has helped me throughout my life. "You reap what you sow."

Benjamin Franklin High School In Harlem

Although I never wanted to be a teacher or a principal, unemployment and eviction notices forced me to take a substitute teacher position at Benjamin Franklin High School in 1978. I taught but I was still searching for a purpose. I went to the North Carolina School of The Arts because I didn't want to work on the farm or in the factories of Scotland County. When I graduated from high school, I wanted to do "something." I was told that I was going to "grow up and be a drunk just like your daddy." My daddy wanted me to be a barber so he could get free haircuts.

Franklin is located in Harlem at 116th Street on FDR Drive. Harlem was not the same city that my cousins from New York had told us about. As a little boy in the South, everyone I had ever seen from New York had big cars, processed hair, fine clothes, lots of money, liquor, latest records, and could dance and laugh a lot. Harlem was supposed to be a Black Mecca or Heaven. My college readings of the Harlem Renaissance and Black Arts Movement had also painted a picture of superheroes boldly speaking truth to the white establishment.

My first assignment at Franklin was to teach English to chronically absent students. Profanity, fights, illiteracy, teen pregnancy, juvenile crime, projects, welfare, crowded classrooms, dropouts, and at risk students was my baptism into the heart and soul of Black America USA. I received a $10,036.00 a year salary, praise, mini successes, and a strong support system that rekindled my faith that I could achieve and succeed in the Big Apple.

The Beauty Of Harlem

The beauty of Harlem is its people, their talent, creativity, love of their heritage and unwillingness to give in to seemingly insurmountable adversity, challenges and hardships. In many ways it remains a mirror reflecting an indefensible tale of two cities. Undoubtedly, New York is a melting pot of extraordinary wealth. The county's educators, museums, restaurants, Broadway, universities, enviable schools, breathtaking architecture are in shameful contrast with obscene poverty, illiteracy, AIDS, crime, illiteracy, hopelessness and disenfranchisement that nervously coexist in the world's greatest city. If you can make it in New York, you can make it anywhere. There is a big difference between making it and merely existing.

Although I never dreamed of being a teacher, my love of students and the fact that I was good at it prompted Franklin's principal Mel Taylor to make me one of the school's drug counselors.

New York City teachers deserve unswerving veneration for their ability to nurture, motivate and educate students from 100 countries. Despite tribal wars and ethnic confrontations, they have created the best education system in the world. Still,

41

despite a twelve billion dollar budget, dedicated quintessential educators, and nurturing caretakers, the education system bleeds the onslaught of poverty, drugs, illiteracy, racism, and a lack of motivation that have decimated millions of poor New Yorkers. Forsaken neighborhoods, blood-sucking con artists and human predators make one question the stability of civilization in urban America. Young valedictorians, salutatorians and resilient students who engage in daily bare-knuckle toe-to-toe brawls for survival have become the city's unsung, courageous heroes. From diamonds in the rough, New York educators create crown jewels.

Caught In A Deadly Shootout

It was a routine day in the city. I drove my collard green 72 BMW 2002 down the Brooklyn section of Atlantic Avenue and made a right turn on Stuyvesant Avenue. Due to a previous break-in, the door handle was in disrepair, the side window was broken, and the used radio had been stolen. I hopelessly cursed the broken air conditioner, rolled down the window and inhaled the pollution, rotting garbage and toxic fumes of Stuyvesant Avenue. As the car approached Dean Street, two black males yelled obscenities at each other on the adjacent crowded street. Both brandished several guns and waved them in a seemingly well-choreographed deadly ghetto montage of jerky motions indicating anger and fury. Flash! Pop, pop, pop! The gunshots mixed with competing music coming from several ghetto blasters added to the deafening sounds of the Big Apple.

I slammed on my brakes, quickly surveyed the cars frozen in front of me and the startled drivers abruptly backing up behind me. Although, I was almost paralyzed with fright, I placed the BMW in reverse, avoided eye contact and made every effort to avoid being one of the approximately 10,000 black men killed or wounded in this country each year.

Unfortunately, one of the two urban predators opted to use my car as a shield and began shooting at his adversary. The other unshaven "gold tooth" young black man continued cursing in a distinct Caribbean accent. My will to live motivated me to drive on the sidewalk in the same manner that I've always held in contempt and disdain when others used the same maneuvers to circumvent traffic jams. The unwanted urban dance of death partner looked as if he were torn between shooting me or the shooter across the street. He opted to pull a baby in a stroller in front of him, knocked the mother down, called the other assailant foul names, and filled the air with the music of a 9mm gun. The rapid fire of an Uzi or AK 47 was returned as New Yorkers hit the sidewalk, knocked over garbage cans, ran red lights, violated the tranquility of senior citizens, and broke windows of locked stores. Startled, spectators screamed as several bullets ripped throughout the body of an elderly black man unable to evade the waltz of bullets choreographed with life defying precision. Scared, I drove my car off the sidewalk and proceeded to the safety and serenity of my Victorian, fenced in home, with an alarm, that was guarded by two 150-pound AKC registered German shepherds. That day the city had drawn sweat, but had not sucked blood out of my body.

The six o'clock news told the story of a man shot to death behind a US postal mailbox immediately after dropping off a letter. Unfortunately, he was killed on his 66th birthday. Flu-like symptoms, headache, vomiting, watery eyes, sick stomach, weak legs, overwhelmed my aching, but living, body. I remember retelling the story to relatives and co-workers. Everyone laughed at me. This is New York. If you can make it here, you can make it anywhere! Grow up!

Punks Not Allowed At
Benjamin Franklin High School

Ronald Searcy, the assistant principal of Benjamin Franklin High School, told me that my task was to teach English reading to "unloved" disruptive students with a history of chronic absenteeism. Everyday I had to maintain the ritual of talking to passive learners "chronically" arriving to class without paper, pencil, books or the will to defeat illiteracy, ignorance and despair. A 100-pound white female senior citizen was successfully working with students across the hall. Yet, I, as a nurturing 25 year old well-mannered and classically trained black male "role model" was ineffective. Something had to give. An apartment eviction notice was sent to me. I needed the job. This is New York. If you can make it here, you can make it anywhere. Acting jobs were not coming in. I had to pay my rent. I could not afford to lose my job. The chaos, profanity, fights, yelling, and sleeping were my ticket to unemployment. One black male in particular had my number. In street language, he had me by the jock and was squeezing my balls at will. He wore his hat, played his radio, and cursed me at will. He moved from the rear, picked his teeth with a toothpick, and called me a "sissy sucker." Naively and politely I asked, "What did you say?" The other students snickered. Without hesitation, he looked in my eyes and uttered a string of four-letter words. I knocked over the trashcan, threw the desk separating us, and unprofessionally yelled. Unemployment, eviction, blood, fist flying, handcuffs, emergency rooms, police, principal, disappointment all rushed through my mind as my blood flushed and my heart pumped. But I was determined to go out with street dignity. You suck up your pride. You may get your ass kicked, but one thing you cannot do is be a punk. City kids teach you a lot. "Life or death, rich or poor." Nobody respects or likes a punk. I could live with losing my job. I would survive unemployment. Ain't no way I was going down as a punk. Teach, fight or die, but as of today, I was reclaiming my authority as the person in charge of my classroom.

44

An oasis of serenity encompassed a seemingly barren desert of distress and hopelessness. The intimidator smiled, took off his hat and the other students picked up papers, straightened up my desk, and applauded. They laughed. Ooh God, how they let out a diaphragmatic gut-wrenching laugh. Suddenly, a young African American female smiled and shouted, "Thank God we finally got a teacher!" The intimidator stayed after class and said, "Mr. Pankey, you know you all right. Understand, right? This is Harlem. You the 10th teacher we've had in three months. We don't want no punk for no teacher." After school, another female student from an honors class came by and said, "I like a strong black man. I think you are so sexy..."

Welcome to Harlem and the real world of the urban educator. I never had another major problem out of the class. My students improved, came to school daily, shared tragic life experiences, and demonstrated extraordinary love and dedication. The level of raw talent was beyond human comprehension. They were excellent writers and incredible speakers. Their poise and charisma exceeded anything I had seen at the N. C. School Of The Arts. They were fascinated with a new art form called "rhyme" or "rap". The students consistently wrote and spoke about dying at an early age. Everyone knew someone who had been murdered. Many were eyewitnesses to murder, beatings, and stabbings. Far too many girls had been sexually molested or raped. Conversations were explicit and uninhibited.

In addition to the traditional New York State English curriculum, my students were required to make two oral presentations. We had negotiated the content. Teachers told me that I would never get them to recite in front of the class. They were wrong, big time! The students would perform Shakespeare's sonnets, contemporary poems, original rhyme or rap. Students would make a strange noise with their lips and often beat on their desks. They had a cockiness and confidence I had never seen before. 100% of the students would perform this new and exciting mixture of poetry, music, rhyme and beating on objects for punctuation of certain sounds or effects.

Although, it started in urban ghettoes, rhyme or rap was exploding throughout the recording and entertainment industry. Sugar Hill Gang, Curtis Blow, Dr. Jekyll & Mr. Hyde were all performing in Harlem's projects. The same was happening all over the city. Something different was happening and little did any of us know that the big black thick records sold out of basements or the trunks of cars would forever change the entertainment industry and American culture. The world was changing. The influence of hard, raw, unapologetic rap would soon change the entertainment industry.

Power Struggles At Hughes High School

My position was cut at Franklin, because of a lack of money. I was sent to Hughes High School in lower Manhattan. At Hughes, I came to understand the impact of a principal. Mr. Leonard Blackman was the principal of a large New York City School that was out of control. The school lacked vision and someone in charge. Students arrived to school late, cut classes, fought and showed a remarkable disdain for adult authority figures. The principal lacked the leadership skills necessary to inspire and command the respect of the school's stakeholders.

While there, I also felt the sting of an assistant principal's arrogance and abuse of power. Periodically, he told New York City police officers to tow my car away at $150.00 a tow. My annual salary in 1980 was about $11,000.00 a year. I was confused, angry and devastated. This seemed especially odd because I had a parking sticker issued from Benjamin Franklin. Later, I heard rumors that the assistant principal requested removal of my car because he had not issued the sticker. The administration and staff at Franklin were kind and supportive. This particular administrator was a horse of another color. This was my first baptism in mean-spirited education bureaucracy and politics. More lessons followed.

I was the director of the school's drug prevention program. The district director told me to lie about the number of active students in my program. His reason was my numbers exceeded those of some of the other directors and it wouldn't look good.

Actually, I was fond of the school's principal. Veteran teachers told me that any association with the principal would be the kiss of death. I didn't have a clue about school politics. During the year, Mr. Blackmon was replaced by James Warren.

Warren's presence dramatically changed the tone of the school. The chaotic environment quickly became a calm education institution. It is amazing what good leadership will do for a school.

Boys And Girls High School's Chancellor

I was invited to do my one-man show at Boys and Girls High School in Brooklyn. Afterwards, I was offered a teaching position there. I took the job at the end of my first year at Hughes. Phillip Cox, a former professional football player, was the school's principal. Boys And Girls High School had about 3,500 students from 45 different countries. Boys And Girls High School was probably the best and worst of urban schools. Most of the students qualified for free lunch. The ongoing power struggle between the United Federation of Teachers and the school's administration overshadowed any possibility of a harmonious work environment.

Frank Mickens became the new principal in the early 80s. Mickens is an articulate, intelligent, street savvy educator from the heart of Brooklyn. He made me the coordinator of school assemblies. During one of the assemblies, I dubbed Boys and Girls High School as the Miracle of 1700 Fulton Street. Mickens is very independent and aggressive. He is a man of uncompromising courage. He defies and shows disdain for traditional educators, administrators, and individuals without heart. The Bedford Stuyvesant grass root community activists, parents, students, clergy and elected officials strongly support his vision for Boys and Girls High School. He connects with the heart and souls of his students. Mickens' son was killed in a car accident at an early age. Mickens is dedicated to ensuring that all 3,500 of his children get a good education.

During his first assembly with students he announced, "My name is Frank Mickens and I'm on a mission." Students cheered. "I'm on a mission" was a very, very popular saying in the ghetto. "Mick" understands the street culture, body language, and this has made him a star with his students.

Mickens publicly questioned the knowledge, integrity and motivation of New York City's Board Of Education officials and was constantly in their doghouse, but Sonny Carson, Al Sharpton, City Councilman Enoch Williams and Assemblyman Al Vann covered his back. He acknowledged the legal Chancellor of the school system, but declared himself the Chancellor of 1700 Fulton Street. He told the District Superintendent to stay in his house and Mick would stay in the house that he built named Boys and Girls High School.

My theatre background gave me the staging and public relations skills often utilized by Mickens. Teachers claimed that he used people. Perhaps Maya Angelou said it best when she stated, "If I can't be used, then I am useless." He simply did what he had to do to run the school. Mickens created an environment that was one of the safest comprehensive high schools in the state. Dress for Success, a safe environment, pride, dignity, and self-respect are the hallmarks of the miracle at 1700 Fulton Street.

Success By Breaking All The Rules

Mickens quickly took several significant steps to make Boys and Girls High School the pride and joy of Brooklyn, New York. He held weekly motivational assemblies, monthly awards programs, and constant public relations events, maintained direct contact with media, solicited support of churches, support of the coaching fraternity, knew thousands of students by their names, demonstrated an incredible memory, ruled as an authoritarian and surrounded himself with loyal people.

The attachment of monthly awards assemblies to PTA meetings dramatically increased attendance for both events. There was a time when less than 10 people attended PTA meetings. By adding an awards program, talent, guest speakers and soul food, attendance increased to over 1,000 per function. This is very significant because it gave parents a sense of empowerment and made Mickens an untouchable icon. New

York City politics changes like the tide of the Atlantic Ocean, but Mick's power base is as constant as the Northern Star.

Dress for Success came about during several meetings we had regarding school uniforms. He was leaning toward uniforms, but I insisted that a simple shirt and tie was the move to make. We intended to have only the senior boys Dress for Success two days a week. Whew! All hell broke loose. I was the senior advisor and angry girls came to my office and wanted to know why I thought only boys could be "successful". We started a seniors only Dress for Success. Eventually, under classmen wanted to participate. Although it took courage, Mickens mandated the program for all students. 100% dressed for success. We checked Dress for Success every Monday and Wednesday. It worked. Mickens received calls from churches, businesses, education leaders and all aspects of the media. Once the story was published in The New York Times, the NFL and other sponsors guaranteed that every student was given two dress shirts and neckties. Surprisingly, girls were eager to wear shirts and ties, too. They also wore dress skirts, dresses, pantsuits, and blouses. Boys wore dress shirts, ties, jackets or suits.

During staged assemblies, I created slogans, "From Diamonds In The Rough to Crown Jewels," "The Miracle of 1700 Fulton Street,"and "Micken's Miracles." Despite my loyalty, stressful tension developed between us. Other staff members lined up to choose sides. Many stated that I had exploited my theatrical training tricks and created a media hungry monster that was out of control. Mickens was a new star in New York City's political and educational environment. Politics and education are one and the same. My respect and admiration of him did not keep him from kicking me out of his inner circle. I had never met a man with the principles of this great principal. Mick was tough. When he did not consider me for the vacant assistant principal position of the English department, I knew that our relationship had soured. Why?

When One Door Closes Another Opens

One evening during the first week of school in 1991, Brooklyn and Staten Island Superintendent Joyce Coppin offered me the interim acting position of assistant principal of English at Tilden High School. Throughout the evening, I reflected upon my 11 years at Boys and Girls High School. I rehearsed what I thought would be an emotional final meeting with Mickens. The meeting lasted approximately one minute. His only comment was "It's time for you to go!" At the faculty conference he stated, "Mr. Pankey will immediately report to Tilden High School as the new Assistant Principal of English." No praise. No other comments. No thanks. Quietly I wondered if our professional ties were cut. I knew my emotional bond, and love and respect for him was everlasting. His courage and philosophical influence would forever steer the sail of the ship that guided my career. Frank Mickens took on the system and fought for Black and Hispanic kids. His focus was on "quality of life issues." He gave incentives, notebooks, paper, pencils, awards, sweat, and tears. He gave it all. We love Frank Mickens!

The Caribbean Revolution At Tilden High School

Tilden High School's interim acting principal, Carol Griffin, summoned me to her office. Her confident demeanor did not mask an unstoppable uprising among Tilden's staff. Its president of the United Federation of Teachers vowed that Griffin's temporary appointment would never become permanent. Carol believed that Tilden was not ready for a Black female principal. Teachers characterized her administrative style as crude, bossy, harsh, and unacceptable. Her leadership style was described as a rudderless ship in shark-infested waters headed toward

50

an iceberg. Leadership is often a matter of finding the best marriage. Carol was a highly skilled administrator, but the staff would not accept or support her as principal.

The overwhelming majority of Tilden's staff was white. The previous principal was a white male. He had held the position for over 20 years. They had never had a Black administrator. Tilden had an enrollment of 2,500 students and 99% were African American Caribbean. There was no love lost between the Jamaican and Haitian pupils.

Despite pleas to the contrary, I held a motivational assembly my first week on campus. I received a thunderous ovation within the first 30 seconds. Again, it hit me that educators consistently misread the culture of teenagers. The Caribbean culture is very passionate. This passion is too often erroneously perceived as hostile and aggressive. Before the assembly, I was candidly told, "These niggers don't know how to act. They are wild coconuts. Do not put these fools together in the auditorium." The tougher I talked, the more the kids applauded. The more zero tolerance rules I mandated, the longer the applause. Mega surprise! Their behavior was almost a mirror image of the ovations Frank Mickens received at Boys and Girls High School. Tough Love was welcomed and appreciated by many students. Love must be fair and discipline has to be consistent and equitable. The media and grapevine will focus on tough, but the substance is love. Mickens and Joe Clark are right! Students disrespect and feel unsafe with punk administrators. I repeated to the students that they were the miracle of New York City public schools and they were the fulfillment of the loftiest dreams of our forefathers. From diamonds in the rough, they had become crown jewels. They were the descendants of kings and queens and "we ain't no joke!"

I walked out of the auditorium with students clapping, stomping their feet and realized that the assembly had turned into a revival with a reaffirmation of pride, dignity, and self-respect. Everyone was in shock, but me. I'd written and acted the same script many times at Boys and Girls. Young people have never let me down!

Tilden was not Boys and Girls High School. Despite having one thousand fewer students, hell broke loose at least once a week. Rival ethnic gangs or community groups kicked royal butt each week. The Haitians and Jamaicans had some fierce fights. Intra-racial hatred created tribal war in the hallways, cafeteria, and on the streets. It was not out of the ordinary for ten or more police cars to surround the school building. A permanent glazier was on staff and stayed busy repairing broken windows each day. This was not the movie or television version of The Black Board Jungle. This was New York. New York schools can be a heaven or hell. It depends on what day it was.

This was another school out of control. During the change of classes, windows were broken, and doors were kicked apart; bilingual racial slurs were the new core curriculum. Still, teachers and the union held fast to their nonsupport of Principal Carol Griffin. It was readily apparent that she did not have enough support to be an effective administrative or instructional leader. We knew her days were numbered. Who would she take down with her? How long could Superintendent Joyce Coppin support her?

School Killing At Jefferson High School

We all became numb when the news flashed that two students had been shot dead in the hallways of Jefferson High School. Jefferson is located approximately three to five miles away from Tilden. Griffin was a close friend of Jefferson's principal Carol Beck. New York's first African American mayor David Dinkins was scheduled to visit the school. Moments before Dinkins was scheduled to speak, pupils became entangled in a fatal confrontation that sent New York's parents, educators, politicians, and students into panic and trauma. Despite the presence of over 30 police officers, the students were killed in the hallways of the school. Although school officials would deny it, guns in school were common. Shootings outside of schools were part of urban life, but shooting in the halls was a new experience. Blood flowing from the temple of two students left a temporary stain on the hallway floors, but implanted permanent images in our heads. America was forced to face the reality of death in a school. We questioned whether

52

or not schools were a safe haven for our children. This was only a premonition of a national epidemic of school killings to follow.

Immediately after the fatal shooting, The New York City Board of Education added millions of dollars to the school's security budget. Some schools were assigned up to 14 security guards and police officers. (They now have up to 35.) School security is now under the control of the New York City Police Department. Police, guards, metal detectors, locker searches, cameras, alarms, iron bars on windows, aides guarding bathrooms, bathroom searches, and clear book bags are permanent fixtures of the system's landscape.

Books, Butts And Bullets

Razors braided into hair, hidden between teeth or behind large belt buckles are the new innovations for smuggling weapons into buildings. Guns and knives are routinely handed in windows. Slipping weapons into the school after hours is a dependable strategy that enables violence prone students to menace "nerds" and good kids. Creative schemes are regularly invented to get around metal detectors. Unfortunately, most educators think like middle-class law-abiding citizens. They refuse to get into the head of juvenile delinquents and human predators. Most students are good most of the time, but about 5 to 10% are a threat to the others. In a system with over one million students, 5 to 10% of potential trouble is the road to hell.

The ever-increasing violence, dropouts, suspensions, assaults on school personnel, low test scores, inability to teach, apathy, and lack of teacher confidence doomed Carol's ability to get the permanent appointment as principal. Consequently, tall, smart, and highly respected W. L. Sawyer received the official appointment as Tilden's first appointed Black principal. Sawyer's Barry White voice, congenial personality, tall physical stature, and excellent rapport with the stakeholders made him an instant star. Tilden's branch of the United Federation

53

of Teachers, students, teachers, parents, staff and community-based organizations were energized by his appointment. Instantly, the school's tone changed for the better.

In the middle of my administrative rookie year as Tilden's assistant principal of the English Department, rumors spread that Dr. Susan S. McKinney's Junior High School 265 interim acting principal Carmella Murden was going to be fired. JHS 265 is located in the midst of the Fort Green housing projects. Fort Green is the 17th largest project in the country. "Bed Sty do or die" was the slogan in the Boys and Girls community. Sty's gang-bangers were afraid of the "Fort". It has one of the highest crime rates in New York. The United Federation of Teachers cited Dr. Susan S. McKinney JHS 265 as New York's fifth most violent school. The word on the street was that my name was circulating as the community's choice to become the next principal. The streets said the new principal was blacker than blue, from down south and meaner than Joe Clark or Mickens. Politics and education are one and the same in New York. I had never heard of the school and didn't know anything about Fort Green. But, I was advised to apply for the position. Apply how? Where? A middle school? Veteran administrators told me to get a grip. "You don't turn down a principal's job." The streets sent me some messages. "We hope you are not hot air." "Nobody can live up to your buildup." "Kick ass Pankey & don't look back!" "Kick ass day one, or you will not be back the second day."

During the spring of 1992, I visited the school. Several students saw me and ran into the cafeteria yelling, "He's blacker and greasier than they said. He be mean. New principal is in the halls! That's him! Lordy, lordy!"

A few weeks before the interview process, two students were shot at the school. They survived. A shooting is usually the kiss of death for a principal. Hot rumors hit the Fort that Murden often retreated to her office and cried in front of staff members. Other news spread that students and parents "cussed her out at will." Community activists and parents roamed the halls in an effort to restore order in the troubled institution. Drugs were openly sold in the school's playground, at the bus stop, and on the adjacent streets. Pit bulls, guns, knives and snakes were used during the robbery of students. My photograph and resume were circulated throughout the community. I saw my photo posted on light poles. I got the job and told New York Newsday

54

that I guaranteed the improvement of the school or I would quit at the end of the first year. I challenged the newspaper to spend a year in the school. They accepted the challenge. "Every child deserves a school that is either successful or en route to success."

The Great Society On Drugs

Fort Greene is a scalding indictment of all that went wrong with Lyndon Johnson's "Great Society." The concept of projects has turned out to be such a tragedy that it couldn't be worse if the "Great Society" was on drugs. What genius thought of putting poor people together in highly populated urban neighborhoods? The overcrowded poor inhabitants are often described as crabs in a barrelful of hot oil. Dreams are stillborn. Life in the ghetto is a dreamless day-to-day existence where fake jewelry, expensive sneakers, rotten meat, overpriced food, and window-rattling music provide temporary relief from drudgery and despair. A few make it out. Most play the survival game of Russian roulette. Nike and Reebok provide the status sneakers; and Spike Lee, Mike Tyson, rap artists, Puff Daddy, Alan Iverson, Sonny Carson and Al Sharpton are the heroes. They tell the truth to white folks with power.

The Truth About Ghetto Children

Ghettoes represent the perfect metaphor of the Great Society on crack. Welfare has created an unmotivated comatose generation of illiterate high school graduates that lack the will or skills necessary to overcome poverty. Murder, teen pregnancy, AIDS, infant mortality, rape, muggings, incest, poverty, ignorance, fear, pain and hopelessness are bleeding cesareans on the pus and maggot-filled infectious blisters of urban blight. Welfare and good intentions gone astray add salt to open wounds. Nine millimeter guns have replaced pacifiers, and sirens are the new lullabies to put babies to sleep. Children sleep on floors because parents are afraid of the bullets that are randomly sprayed through windows each night. The "411" or "word on the street" is that teenagers have made verbal wills and put caskets on layaway so they can go out in style! Weekend death tolls are listed each Monday in the daily tabloids. Students come to school on Mondays talking about who got killed, put in jail, beat up, or busted for drugs over the weekend. Old men screw young girls and boyfriends spend the night on couches in homes that are usually missing a daddy. The gossip queens spread bad news before the newspapers get the facts wrong. Teachers periodically scratch names off attendance rolls and reassign seats. Funerals are short. Graves are narrow. Tears dry up fast. Ghetto children have an incision sewn into their smiles and frowns. But they are still children! Rich and poor are equally stressed out in an over-populated city that has the best and worst the world has to offer.

New York City is a classic tale of two cities. Limousines and gypsy cabs park side by side. Wall Street and abandoned graffiti decorated buildings that serve as shoot up galleries and cheap whorehouses or shelter for the homeless are only separated by city blocks and the imagination. Young children and urban educators are the invisible heroes of the city. The budget for the New York City Board of Education exceeds 12 billion dollars. We trust our money and children to big spenders that pay custodians more than principals and teachers.

Principal With Principles

Dr. Susan S. McKinney JHS 265's staff slowly, methodically, and cautiously approached me with the fight night jitters of a heavyweight boxing match. Dennis Hinson, the only assistant principal and the three coordinators, Helen Henderson, Sharyn Hemphill and Eddie Corbett, were supportive and excited about my arrival as the new principal.

Teacher assistant and community activist Louise Hallett was an immediate and permanent supporter throughout my administration. Slowly the staff embraced a country boy from the cotton and tobacco fields of North Carolina. Although reluctantly optimistic, they appeared to be in a semi-traumatic state that one would expect from tired, weary, and shell-shocked Vietnam War veterans. They were starving for structure and bold leadership.

Prior to the first orientation assembly with students, we vehemently reviewed zero tolerance, security, and discipline procedures. Students were mandated to quietly lineup and proceed to the auditorium in a no-nonsense, orderly fashion. Staff members and security were strategically placed along the passageway and in the auditorium. Of course, earlier that morning, I shined my shoes, ironed my shirt, and wore my best suit and tie for this critical first meeting. I shook the hand of every student.

Fight For Territory

Suddenly, a young, 15-year old African American male dressed in a rugged, beige full-length lambskin, shearling jacket, gold teeth, rings on 8 fingers, and a braided gold chain yelled, "Yo yo yo yo, yawl niggers look like fools. That nigger done housed ya'll. Nigger got ya in check!" My mouth became dry; the side of my head was throbbing and pulsating. I felt blood rushed through my body. All my years at Boys And Girls, Benjamin Franklin, Hughes and Tilden High schools had taught me that the minute you punk out, you forever lose your school. This was the deciding moment.

Dreary and boring hours of studying at universities never prepared me for a new generation of cold, heartless adolescents raised with a brick hard dog-eat-dog street mentality, breast-fed and weaned with the survival of the fittest philosophy. The marching harmonious ensemble of students froze to watch my swan song as he attempted to reaffirm his control of territory.

Can't Punk Out

Dammit, I had picked cotton, picked beans, smelled musk, wiped sweat in 100-degree weather and then worked as a lowly paid substitute teacher for years. The fading hopes, dreams, aspirations, and ritualistic disappointment in everyone's eyes began piercing through my body like an X-ray machine cultivated in the intestinal walls of Hades. One moment in time was about to destroy my vision of a "Prep School." It doesn't have to be that way! I ain't gonna go down that way! I will lose my school if he takes this priceless moment. Bourgeois or street! Go middle class and I will not hit the ground running! I will just hit the ground. Yet, I will lose my job if I go street! Either way I lose. If I use education vernacular, everyone will laugh and the middle school in the procession will erupt in an outburst of chaos and laughter. Imagine the screams. "We are going to tear this mother down. Woof, woof, tear the roof off the mother. Party! Party!"

Using the rage of Walter Lee from A Raisin in the Sun, I screamed, "What did you say?" He directed an endless barrage of vulgarities and bumped me. Instantaneously, I grabbed him by the shoulders, spun him around, put him in a headlock and dragged him out of the hall and into my office. Throughout this process I lectured. "I am not a nigger. I am the principal. Let me make one thing very, very clear. You have two choices. You can come to school and obey the rules like everyone else or you can get a suspension to go home. You got no juice in my school. You take this to the streets; the man with the juice is Pankey. I am the principal! I am not afraid of you! We are taking back our school. We got new rules. You live by them or go to school someplace else."

He screamed, "Nigger you gonna die!" I responded, "Then I will die, but I ain't giving up my school. My name is Mr. Pankey. I am the principal and you are a child. We make the rules. You follow them. You do what you feel you gotta do and I will do what I gotta do. You got no juice here. Take it to the streets! A man's gotta do what a man's gotta do." Physically, he offered

58

STANDING IN THE SHADOWS OF GREATNESS

very little resistance, but verbally he responded in descriptive expletives and vowed to come back with his homeboys and tools. As he ran out the side door, he yelled, "I am coming back with my mama. She gonna dog you!"

Sweating, heart pounding, hot, frustrated and feeling shocked and embarrassed by a lowly lack of professionalism that had assaulted my ethics and crashed my moral compass, I walked into the school's auditorium. Perhaps I had lost my job?

Ain't Nothing Gonna Turn Us Around

Ear piercing thunderous applause and revival Holy-Ghost-like foot stomping greeted me. I hid my embarrassment by doing an impression of Muhammad Ali. I ran to the podium. Grabbed the microphone and began my declaration that we are gonna turn this school around:

"The party is over. I hope everybody had fun the last ten years, because I am here to send a message to the living, dead and yet unborn that we have come to announce the resurrection of knowledge, wisdom and understanding at Dr. Susan S. McKinney JHS 265. From diamonds in the rough, you will become crown jewels. You are the miracle of 101 Park Avenue, Fort Green, Brooklyn, New York State, the nation, and perhaps the world. You are not a dream deferred, but the fulfillment of our loftiest dreams and aspirations. You are what Dr. King was talking about when he said I am not worried about anything, I am not fearing any man...mine eyes have seen the glory. You are that glory. I am so proud to be the new principal of 265. I will not let you down! In the words of our forefathers, ain't nothing gonna turn us around. You come from greatness. Greatness is your birthright. We are on the move now. Nobody will ever look down on you again. It is a new day. It is a new school. You are the best. You are the greatest. You are the most morally sound, ethical, creative, and intelligent committed group of young people to ever walk the planet earth, second to none.....Let me say to you, and I will say it again and again and again, I will see you at the top!"

59

An old fashioned revival broke loose. The only thing missing was the old ladies with wigs on sideways, fried chicken and lemonade. But we had the weaves! The shouting started. The dancing in the aisles erupted. Students and teachers were crying! Kids ran to the front of the stage and started dancing with me. I did my best James Brown imitation and prayed my pants hadn't split. Then, they started yelling, "Go Pankey, go Pankey, go Pankey!" Parents hugged me. An elderly black woman squeezed me and sobbed. "Martin Luther! Martin Luther! I have waited my whole life for this moment. This school's been hell for years. Where you been? I can now die happy. God sent you here. God is working through you. You the one. I can now die happy. Martin Luther King, Jr.! Martin Luther has come back! Shout it up to the mountaintops! Martin Luther! Martin Luther! Jesus! Jesus! Jesus! Thank you Jesus!"

Helen Henderson stated that she had worked at the school for 30 years and prayed for this day. Eddie Corbett picked up my coat and dusted it off. Dennis Hinson restored order and redirected students to their second period class. His final comments were, "We finally got a principal with principles!"

Throughout the day students hugged me. Oh, we had our typical urban middle school verbal altercations and the drug dealers, thugs, and muggers brazenly came on the school's playground each lunch period to stake their "territorial rights." The first day ended without a major fight.

Students and staff went home. Only the custodians and I remained. Around 5:00 p.m., I went back into the auditorium. My wrinkled and rumpled clothes were now wet and sticking to my body. Yes, I had split my pants. Thank God I kept my jacket on all day. I was full of doubt. The expectations were high.

I sat in the auditorium for hours. I stared at the torn curtains, dirty carpet, broken lights and stained glass windows. I cried. I prayed. I thought and thought. For years, I have carefully practiced articulation, studied Stanislavski Acting, stage presence, speaking, writing, karate in preparation for a career as an actor. What in the hell am I doing here? Be careful what you pray for! For years, I had asked God for an opportunity to leave the rural Pankey Town community, pigs, outdoor toilets, and emptying the slop jar full of pee. My mind raced back to the days when we were called coons, colored, Negroes, country,

Afro Americans or Black and read old books white kids didn't want. The video express in my head recalled Carver High School, leaking roofs and sleeping on floor pallets. My daddy going to the chain gang and feeling his rough beard rubbing against my face during holiday visits. I remembered our school bus drove by him on the chain gang and everyone laughed. The ammonia smell of liquor on his breath each Christmas day. The stomach cramps I had due to hunger. I thought of the power company turning the lights out. I remembered the burning of candles instead of electricity. Cold. No coal. No firewood. Gotta go in the snow 'cause ya forgot to cut wood. Oh, and doing the nasty under the porch. Just remembering the old days in Pankey Town. From Pankey Town to Fort Green? It doesn't have to be this way. Lord, this place has been an urban target practice and drug infested testing lab for years. How could this school be in the richest city in the world? Lordy, Lordy, Lordy, please help me!

Taking Back The School

When I was appointed principal of Dr. Susan S. McKinney JHS 265, it was considered to be unmanageable. The school had a history of violent and disruptive students and parents. The tougher I talked, the more students cheered and embraced me. School was school, again. Teachers laughed and kids played in the playgrounds. Tough, benevolent discipline was accepted by the school stakeholders. Hell, if I can make it here, I can make it anywhere. My God, the system, America has grossly underestimated poor Black and Puerto Rican children and perhaps all low-achieving disruptive kids. They want the basics described in Maslow's hierarchy of needs.

First, the children want a daddy to provide for and protect them from the bad guys, and there are bad guys who will hurt children. They yearn for a strong, consistent, fair, humanistic and benevolent disciplinarian with an unswerving affinity for all children. Tough Love-Unconditional Love without expecting anything back! They want a bully willing to literally fight, teach, guide, and nurture them. The stakeholders at the school were tired of the same old bourgeois rhetoric and politics as usual. They had already wrestled and lost their fight with the devil. They gave up on principals who gave up on them. They don't want a principal in name only. If you just looking for a job or want to pity someone, don't work here. Now, they have upped the ante. They want a Messiah or at the minimum a PRINCIPLE.

Education Malpractice

Hollywood's stereotypical depiction of urban schools has rarely shown the raw courage of classroom teachers. Perhaps, they are motivated by some unknown divine intervention. Prior to my arrival, teachers and staff often needed police escorts at the end of bloody and grueling days. Typically, when students fought, whole families came to the school and joined the fray. Disputes with the administration, teachers, or staff were handled by family or community vigilantes. Street justice reigned supreme. Often, older high school siblings, dropouts, or whoever had the most juice (crazy people), home boys, or home girls settled disputes.

Realistically, it's one thing to ask for a tough-ass principal, but it's another ballgame to teach marketable skills, reading, writing, character education, math, and science. Literacy is the name of the game. A declaration of war on ignorance and the teaching of core middle class values is the mission of school. Credibility is a serious problem, because poor children see a tale of two school systems. They observe wealthy celebrities and millionaire drug dealers coexist with minimum wage teachers that they are supposed to respect. Parents work at jobs they despise and constantly talk of racism and harassment by the boss. Mortgages are 30 years of debt. Life in the projects is hell, but welfare and Medicaid are dependable. College takes four years. The future looks like a lay-away plan with fluctuating interest rates.

In essence, school seems to be a con job and is a hard sell. Chalk and talk compete with Jerry Springer, Ricki Lake, Tupac, and Dennis Rodman, getting high, sex and rap music. Urban youth perceive education as white-like. They hate the white middle class and hold incinerated hot coals in their hearts and souls for the rich. They are jealous of celebrities and don't have the slightest idea what to make of "buppies"or "yuppies."

Learning to read in middle or high school is the ultimate embarrassment and carrying notebooks ain't cool. Naively, my first order of business was mandating notebooks. Okay, I caught on! "The notebook must have paper in it!" Baggy pants without belts were worn so low that when the wind blew the butts whistled! Missing shoestrings was the style. Razors in braids or hidden behind the tongue, dyed hair, gold teeth, shirttails hanging out, marijuana glazed eyes, sex without condoms, clown-like make up, walkmans, CD players, beepers, and two cell phones were the norm. Cussing teachers out was the joint. Dogging an administrator was the ultimate status symbol. But my soul was uplifted every time I saw a student raise his or her hand to answer a question or give me an essay or poem to read. The innocent, the smart, the hunger in their eyes, smiles, hugs and sharing of candy, and the incredible work ethics of teachers energized me every day. I arrived to work early and left late. I couldn't wait to see my crown jewels each day. My daily emotions were torn between joy and disappointment. It is education malpractice to not provide a quality education for all children.

My lunch duty initiation involved witnessing a ritual that entailed putting tables together to create a stage so everyone could watch a fight. Part of the day consisted of watching drug dealers accompanied by pit bulls, pet snakes, robberies or acts of intimidation directed toward students and staff. The New York City Board of Education owned the building, but drug dealers and gang bangers owned the schoolyard and psyche of many kids.

Ed Corbett was one of the department coordinators. He was a tall, light-skinned, slim, soft spoken and religious man whose faith sustained him for years at 265. His faith in God eliminated his fears. As my mentor, I watched him stare down drug dealers and take beaten kids away from neighborhood bullies. Corbett took guns away from kids and ran pit bulls, winos, addicts and miscreants off campus with the calmness of a monk. Often I inquired how our school could be a dumping ground for School District 13's troubled youth. He calmly said that that's the way it has always been. Other seasoned veterans often chimed in that District 13 had decided that certain schools would house the gifted and talented, but the troubled souls were sent to project schools. One of 265 sub schools included the gifted and talented housed at Satellite West in a location approximately one half miles away. But conventional wisdom had it that 265 was a ghetto school. The school had one copier. Requests for copies were sent to the central office and we often waited a week for their return. Students were not given books to take home and there were half enough books for each student in classes. Books were shared. I had to write letters requesting no more than one hundred postage stamps at a time. Sometimes stamps were denied or my messengers were verbally abused. New York City schools have gifted and talented children, but some are perceived and treated as stepchildren. Even in a school system with a 12 billion dollar budget, these conditions exist. That's just the way it is!

Shortchanging Poor Students

There are rich schools and there are poor schools. At the time, the New York City Board Of Education had a budget of 12 billion dollars. Dr. Susan S. McKinney JHS 265 did not have the following:

100% fully licensed teachers
Books for all students
A copier machine
Working computer lab
Calculators
Band equipment or uniforms
Postage stamps
Auditorium curtains
Working lights or sound system in the auditorium

Updated library books
School librarian
Active PTA
Curriculum aligned with standardized tests
Pacing guides
Benchmark tests
Highly qualified teachers

Blueprint For Success

The dealers owned the playgrounds and everyone knew it. We often called the police, but no one responded. In the absence of leadership, none of the advocates for children had taken command. Seriously, I was adamant that the party was over. Drug dealers, dogs, bullies, snakes, guns or other weapons were no longer allowed on campus. How do you enforce the rules? First, we are going to send a message that it is our schoolyard!!! Heads up! Straight up and down we are gonna deal with it. We will take back our classrooms, halls, cafeteria, park and school! I taught my assistant principal and coordinators the concept of W. E. D. G. E.

Walk Around Every Day To Guarantee Excellence:
Require effective classroom instruction
Model high expectations
No excuses
Be visible
Stay in the halls during the passing of classes
Cover the cafeteria all lunch periods
Eat with students
Develop good relationships
Monitor classroom instruction everyday
Greet students every morning
Meet students at the buses in the morning
Walk to the cars and greet parents
Check notebooks
Inspect dress

Check for homework in the halls, cafeteria and classrooms
Walk students to the buses in the afternoon
Carefully supervise students at all times
Walk, talk and get to know everyone by his or her names
Be courageous
Lead

Heads up! Effective immediately, the following rules
are mandatory:
Notebooks
Paper and pencil
Shirts tucked in
Pants worn with belts above the waist
No backs, butts or breast showing
No profanity
Shoes tied
Walk to the right
Silent hall passing
No yelling in the halls
Walk in a straight line
Pick up trays and food after eating
Line up when the lunch bell rings
Dress for Success two days a week
No hats worn in the building
Obey the rules
We will consistently enforce our discipline code
The adults are in charge
We run the school

Although resistant, teachers assisted with hall patrols. The assistant principal, coordinators, and security officers were loyal, and dedicated saints throughout my tenure at the school. If the building got too noisy, I ordered "lockdown" and classes were not allowed to travel. Teachers went to each classroom. This was feasible because middle school students were assigned to homerooms that gave each student the same schedule. Weekly or daily motivational speeches were given during regular school assemblies. Mr. Corbett, security officers, and I escorted students to the bus stops, waited for them to leave, and then we cleared the surrounding streets each day. You miss a day or arrive late, then, you hear about a fight. No ifs, ands, or buts, unsupervised students would fight every day. Violence during the day was dramatically reduced. Students saved their fights for after school or on the walking routes home. Weekends and days before long holidays are big city fight days.

Pit Bull Shot On Campus During Fight

Slowly more and more students bought into the "diamonds in the rough crown jewel theory," but older kids from outside the school weren't "going for it!" Consequently, a neighborhood troublemaker known as Big Boy and his friend continued to bring their pit bulls on campus. A female police officer tried counseling him about the dangers of mixing dogs with school kids on campus. He responded by hitting her in the face and letting the dogs loose. He proclaimed that he was from the "Fort" and no one was going to "diss" him.

He talked trash. He stated, "Country nigger, I will kick your ass, her ass, or bust a cap in anybody else's ass if they get in my way." They let the dogs loose! She popped his knees with her nightstick. Once on his knees, she continued working his arms, shoulders, neck and head. Despite spouting blood, a split lip and a broken nose, she continued her onslaught with the acumen of a well-trained martial arts expert. Police officers in backup cruisers arrived within minutes, but the dogs were already running toward the students. Another officer shot one dog in the right paw. It ran into the crowd of students. About ten police officers ran on the schoolyard with their guns drawn. Students, kids, police, gunshots and a bleeding pit bull were beyond the imagination of my worse nightmare. Eventually, the police shot all the dogs and arrested Big Boy.

Surprisingly, very little about the incident was written in the next day's newspapers. I didn't get one call about it. Jet magazine ran a blurb, but didn't mention the name of the school or city. In a city with 8 million people, the killing of a wounded pit bull on a ghetto schoolyard was not newsworthy? Seemingly, the incident would mar the fragile newfound confidence and damage the psyche of the adolescents, but the next day business went on as usual. Nobody mentioned the event. Most of my students had already seen fatal shootings by the time they reached middle school.

Unconditional Commitment To Success

During formal observations, I discovered that many teachers did not speak fluent English and were lacking the minimum teaching credentials necessary for full licensure. Research documents that poor students are often assigned inadequately trained instructors. This can create significant comprehension problems. Elementary school students emulate the enunciation and speech patterns of their adult models. With great despair, I watched a science teacher struggle with basic grammar and standard American speech patterns. Students were irritated, slept, played, squirmed in their seats until a young lady screamed, "Dammit, speak English. Mr. Pankey, suspend me. I can't take it anymore. It ain't fair. They know these teachers can't teach. They think we are stupid." It was my perfunctory duty to take her to the principal's office. She leaned on my chest and cried uncontrollably. "Mr. Pankey, please help us. I got two teachers who don't speak no English. I can't take it no more. Kids be acting stupid. Ain't nobody gonna learn nothing. We gonna flunk those tests and then everybody be talking about how we be dumb. I ain't going back in there. Suspend me. I don't care. I'll drop out before I let that fool teach me. You gotta help us. None of us gonna get into good high schools. We not stupid!"

A 13-year old had just laid out an education malpractice indictment of a school system entrusted with the lives and future of over one million students. A school principal must be an advocate for children. I knew my shaky truce with the chairwoman of the United Federation of Teachers would come to an end. These incompetents had to go. Unconditional Love was a rusty saber that needed its edges sharpened to protect me as I started the necessary paper trail required for the removal of unsatisfactory teachers. Someone must fight for children.

Children cannot fight for themselves. A large amount of energy was expended disciplining pupils, but the new agenda involved holding adults accountable for academic outcomes and student achievement. Who will discipline adults? What are the consequences?

The administrators and I adopted the Best Practices of Effective Schools as established by noted educator Ron Edmonds:

A safe and orderly environment
Climate of high expectations for all students
Competent instructional leadership
Clear and focused mission
Opportunities to learn and student time on task
High visibility-frequent monitoring of student progress
Improvement of home school relationships

Teachers were mandated to write measurable learning objectives directly aligned with the New York State's Standard Course of Study or curriculum. New York City's Chancellor observed that city schools were not teaching the same thing. A citywide effort was underway to standardize the curriculum, but the teachers union was winning the battle to make lesson plans optional. Despite rampant chaos in many schools, site-based management teams were also chipping away regulations requiring teachers to perform hall patrols or cafeteria duties. Disgruntled teachers were winning grievances. Further, New York City principals are not allowed to supervise custodians. Head custodians made up to $85,000.00, beginning teachers made $25,000, and principals made between $65 and $85,000. Various unions were embroiled in turf wars and salary negotiations, but student achievement in poor neighborhoods took a back seat to politics and power struggles. Everybody in the system, but the kids has a union. Far too many of us have taken on the role of the Greek chorus. We are Standing in the Shadows of Greatness!

Children should not be denied all the joys of childhood and growing up. So, we decided to have a celebration of Halloween. Over 100,000 New York City students skip school on "witches' day," and wreak havoc throughout Queens, Manhattan, Staten Island, The Bronx, and Brooklyn boroughs. Newspaper headlines chronicled the killings, shootings, fights, stabbings, property damage, and physical injuries associated with Halloween. My position was 265 was a safe and orderly environment. We invited outsiders and the press to celebrate with us. Of course, many staff members were against this idea, but the little child hiding in adults was eager to come out and play. New York Newsday wrote our story with a headline entitled, "Tough Assignment." It ran a subtitle, "Principal is in Charge at 265."

The published report informed the world that our campus was the model of a safe and orderly environment. In addition to supportive testimonials, the article provided evidence that the school was now a student-friendly sanctuary that afforded teachers an opportunity to teach. As expected, other news stories talked about the M-80 firecrackers exploding throughout the rest of the city. Cherry bombs and acid filled eggs were tossed on unsuspecting bystanders. The death toll throughout the city was high. But our students at 265 were able to enjoy a holiday that they dared not celebrate in the past. Dr. Susan S. McKinney JHS 265 had become the pride and joy of Brooklyn, New York!

Throughout the year I empowered the staff to take back the school. I also encouraged them to take back our homes and communities as well as the hearts and souls of our children; grant every child the sacred gift of childhood. Although, we continued to have discipline problems, most physical fights took place off campus or across the streets. We had taken violence out of the school. The students took it to the streets.

Fighting Ain't Over, Yet

Street fighting is a sick hedonistic immorality play depicting razors slicing aesthetically rich young skin, bottles reshaping teeth, blades piercing skin, bodies greased for slippage, changing from shoes to sneakers, and bloodthirsty crowds cheering gladiators to victory or defeat. Most fights end with the words, "It ain't over, yet!" The sequels often include mothers, fathers, uncles, aunts, brothers, sisters, and sometimes residents of buildings or blocks. The goal is to send the other person into their second life. Fights are motivated by history, memory, stares, accents, clothes, addresses, beauty, ugliness, name calling, race, socio-economics, grades, boredom, and "I don't know." The list is endless. Rarely are they over. You know one thing for sure. You fight. Kick butt or everybody wants a piece of you. If you get a reputation as a punk, you create problems for school administrators. You are food for the maggots if you hit the sidewalk during a fight. Then everybody, including friends, stomp you. Anyone can join a fight. You also better carry a tool (weapon) or be the only fool without one. Bullies carry weapons and smart students afraid of bullies carry a piece. It's the style to carry or know where you can "cop." Pushing up daisies ain't no joke. Revolvers are like stupid money, 45's are lukewarm, but Uzi's are cool, word up on the AK 47's, and Tech 9 millimeters! The Glock is hot! It's smart to have a second in the cut (backup gun on your body) so you won't get smoked. If you get it on, you better bring it hard and bring the noise!

The nerds and honor roll students passively coexist with an unruly small core of dysfunctional adolescents. Pupils model the behavior of adults raised in an environment where the loudest, meanest, best fighter or toughest is used as street muscle. Gotta get paid! Gotta survive! Gotta live! Ain't nothing going on but the rent!

Unsung heroes and extraordinary educators daily go to work past the homeless, cutthroat predators, the rich, the famous, educated, uneducated, connected and disenfranchised addicted to and enslaved by a materialistic war fought between heaven and whatever lies between. The working stiffs, middle class, rich and super rich ride trains or subways into a city with eight million dreams and unlimited opportunities.

Perhaps today is the day you hit the numbers or lotto. You can strike it rich in the City. If you can make it here, you can make it anywhere. New York, New York. The Big Apple! New Yorkers are impregnated with the twin passions of optimism and pessimism. Without warning or much fanfare, either will cause real New Yorkers or wannabees to be consumed by narcissistic self-consummation.

Most students attend school every day. They are sometimes actively engaged in a vague undefined phenomenon called higher order thinking skills. These one million experiments from over 100 different countries are truly the unsung heroes of an education bureaucracy in search of identity. Clearly, the front line educators are saints. They can take a ship and make it sail on dry land.

The principal must fight, too. Urban schools need smart, competent and courageous leaders. Everyone will stand around and watch the principal during a fight. However, if you jump into the melee, others will support your efforts. Ed Corbett, Dennis Hinson, security offices Clarence Cooper and Juanita Bridges and I were the first ones to jump into the middle of fights. Urban principals must display courage. You maintain eye contact. You don't look back. You never look away or retreat. Courage is not something you fake. It is a good idea to keep several suits, shirts and ties in your closet. You will get blood on your clothes. You don't complain and nobody feels sorry for you.

You win the respect of the staff, students and parents when you display courage. Some days you will need a police escort to your car. The downside of me being a high profile tough urban principal included the following:

> Car windows shot out
> Car windows smashed
> Graffiti on car/home
> Tires slashed
> Car sitting on bricks at the end of the day
> Car stolen
> Car vandalized
> Cursed
> Death threats
> Stolen radio
> Reputation as the crazy principal

I found cheap tires for $15.00 each. Local merchants would give me discounts. I was able to find cheap car windshields. I had two cars. One car was for work and the other was for the weekends. Many administrators drive a $500.00 principal's car to work and keep their good car at home.

Winning The War

The local media and community supported some of our efforts to create an effective school. During Black History Month in 1993, I called an assembly and declared the school a "prep" school. I gave a speech and told the students that from this day forward they were expected to act like prep school students. Analogies were made with the struggles our forefathers have made throughout history:

"We have waited for this day for over 400 years. It is easy to stand tall when you are standing on someone else's shoulders. We are standing on Madame C. J. Walker, Rosa Parks, Marcus Garvey, Martin Luther King, Jr., Malcolm X, Moses and Jesus. We cannot fail now. Our forefathers are turning over in their graves when they see us using drugs, having illegitimate babies, fighting, cursing, dancing in the streets and putting on "coon" shows. Dream of the day when the whole world will rejoice at the new crown jewel of Fort Green projects, Dr. Susan S. McKinney JHS 265 "Prep" School."

Then, I energetically preached from the words of Dr. Benjamin Mays:

"It must be borne in the mind that the tragedy of life doesn't lie in not reaching your goal. The tragedy lies in having no goal to reach. It isn't a calamity to die with dreams unfulfilled, but it is a calamity not to dream. It is not a disaster to be unable to capture your ideal, but it is a disaster to have no ideal to capture. It is not a disgrace not to reach the stars, but it is a disgrace to have no stars to reach. Not failure, but low aim is sin."

"We want a prep school! We want it here. We want it now. We want it yesterday. Your forefathers have worked, sweated, cried, prayed and died for the day for you to have a prep school. We can't let them down. Ain't nothing gonna turn us around!"

The band played and the chorus sang. Olympic gold medals and other awards were given to the staff. One veteran teacher sobbed uncontrollably and through her tears confided that she had worked over 25 years and no one had ever given her any type of recognition. My God, every budget should include

73

awards and incentives. It just doesn't have to be this way. This is wrong and demoralizing for a school and its personnel. Her testimony is typical of the institutionalization of insensitivity.

Although it was controversial, I felt it was worth the risk because of the perception that our school and its students were doomed to failure. What if public schools adopted the academic vision of private schools? What if poor students were convinced that they were elite prep school scholars? What about a rich academic vision, morals, a safe environment, Afro-centric uniforms, Sunday go to church clothes, quality teaching, and young enthusiastic focused scholars? Why not? I declared 265 a prep school.

Helen Henderson is a 35-year veteran of JHS 265. She's a respected and a tireless teacher-coordinator. Ms. Henderson has integrity beyond reproach and was my most dependable "go-to-person" for advice. Knowing that she had both feet firmly planted on solid rock and acutely aware that my creative instincts often went haywire, I accepted her recommendation to have a kitchen cabinet composed of seasoned political and educationally astute advisors. Helen Henderson, Dennis Hinson, Sharyn Hemphill, Louise Hallett, Clarence Cooper, Ed Corbett and Juanita Briggs were loyal and dependable advisors.

Henderson often beamed and confided that she never thought she would see the day when Black boys would wear shirts and ties at the school. Dress for Success Days were very popular. Kids don't fight when they are dressed up. However, it is the nature of kids to rebel against adult authority figures, but their newfound pride was personified by majestic struts through the hallways like thoroughbreds or feline jungle queens. Privately, student confessed they loved the new dress code.

We consistently checked notebooks, observed classes, monitored the environment and were rewarded by increased test scores, a reduction in violence and fewer suspensions than any middle school in District 13. Success is not a mystery. Although, the powerful United Federation of Teachers did not allow us to mandate the format of lesson plans, we strongly encouraged the Best Practices established by the New York City Board Of Education:

The Criteria Of An Excellent Lesson
*Measurable Learning Objectives Based
on the Standard Course of Study*

Written objective:
Understood by students
Adhered to during the lesson
Referred to during the lesson
Developed out of motivation
Elicited from students
Review of Previous Knowledge
Review of other lessons
Build on what students already know
No unnecessary items included

Routine:
Class starts on time
Students used to distribute papers
Boards erased
Pupils work up to the last minute
Homework is on the board when students arrive
Desks are cleared of extraneous materials
Light and ventilation are good

Motivation:
Pupils are familiar with the phrases and terms involved
Presentation is on the level of pupils
The motivation prepares the way for new lesson
It creates interest-challenges pupils-arouses excitement
It makes use of life experiences of pupils and their families

Drill:
On subject matter of the lesson
Written on the board
On higher level or in different context
With check for the accuracy of the answers
With check to discover which students made errors
Oral and written
Well graded
Adequate
With evidence of mastery by pupils

Presentation of New Materials:
Graded problem work
Logical and sequential development
Pupil understanding of the meaning of terms used
All main entries discussed to be on the board
Outlines on the board

Summary:
Medial summaries provided
Summary of board work
Final summaries provided
Summary related to written objective on the board
Summary in notebooks
Approach different from original development. Not a mere restatement of pivotal questions, "What did we learn today?' is still a good technique.
Widespread pupil participation.
Students summarize lesson.

Homework:
Relevant and used to enrich instruction.
On the board at the beginning of the period
Reasonable in length and difficulty
Outgrowth of the lesson
Graded with optional or bonus work for some
With anticipation and discussion of difficulties by teacher
Motivated
Allotted adequate time for copying
Collected
Returned in a timely manner

Teacher:
Pupil-teacher rapport. Pleasant classroom atmosphere
Encouragement, compliments to pupils with good answers
Knowledge of student's name
Sympathy, patience, consideration, friendliness
Good control of class
Voice audible in all parts of the room
Sense of humor
No tension in the class

Standard use of English
Good voice and clear enunciation
Enthusiasm and vitality

Providing For Individual Differences:
Inspection of written work
Questions directed at those who failed to understand earlier.
    (Follow-up of poor response.)
Offer to help individual members of the group
Inattentive pupil called upon again
Difficult questions directed at better students

Pupil Participation:
Full response should be required. Students required to
    speak in sentences.
Written work at seats
Students writing at board
Students addressing their answers to the class
Students working at the board during the period
Cooperative learning
Wide distribution of questions. Pupils telling about their
    personal experiences related to the lesson
Occasional request to students to stand and to project
Student answers to pupil questions
Pupil questions
Students interested and attentive

Questioning:
Posing of the question before a student is called upon
    for the response. Question (pause) pupil
Calling on both volunteers and non volunteers
Proper assortment of drill and thought provoking questions.
Questions clearly stated.
Thought provoking questions

Avoidance of Poor Questioning Techniques:
Questions requiring a yes or no answer
Number of consecutive questions to one pupil
Leading and tugging questions
Answers repeated

Answers rephrased
Chorus responses
Double questions
Telling, not eliciting
Questions repeated
Questions rephrased

Visual Aids:
Materials on side boards visible to the entire class
Use of other objective material-book, newspaper chart
Blackboard work showing evidence of careful training
Blackboard showing clear flow of development
Updated effective use of technology
Films, slides and power point, etc.
Visibility

Evidence of Planning:
Lesson plans are written
Plans are available for inspection
Use of Lesson Plans
Teacher introduction of illustrative material
Enrichment of the pupil's vocabulary
Plans include interactive strategies
Plans provide assessment instruments

Results:
Learning objective realized
Proper attitudes and skills developed
Knowledge imparted
Evidence of student achievement

Warm Up:
A warm up learning objective
Review of answers
Smooth and brisk transitions
Immediate student engagement
Timing:
Learning objective understood at the beginning
    of the lesson
Sufficient time allotted for review, drills, application
    and development.

Measurement of Results:
Written
Verbal
Show of hands
Completion of products
Did students learn?
How do you know?

Published and word of mouth reports circulated that we had moved from the fifth most violent school in the city to a safe and orderly environment. Many aspects of school improvement were documented by a six-page New York Newsday story entitled Principal Teaches A Fourth R...Respect. The April 11, 1993 story was written by Edna Negron. Photojournalist John Naso had taken over 3,500 photographs of the transition. Challenging the newspaper to stay in the school for a year had paid off! I was not naive. Failure was not an option. I had confidence in my students and staff, and they had a piece of history to prove it! An unrestricted newspaper in a public school was unprecedented.

Although community residents were excited, we never received much praise from the District 13 central office or the Board of Education. However, District 18's superintendent, Dr. Harvey Garner sent me a letter of congratulations and concluded, "A star is born!" Several complimentary stories were written during my tour of duty at JHS 265.

Fame has its price. After each positive news story, rumors, bickering and political infighting threatened my administration. Three different superintendents did not help our cause. The New York City Council of Supervisors and Administrators gave us the "Effective Leadership=Effective Schools" award. Awards and honors continued. I lost track of my awards and letters of commendation.

Although I've never used drugs, drunk alcohol, smoked or was a heavy eater, my body was succumbing to mental, emotional and physical fatigue. My doctor ordered me to stay in bed for one week. He stated that my body was shutting down. If I refused, he was going to place me in the hospital. We were winning the war, but my body was losing the battle. The research and writings of Napoleon Hill became my constant companion. Hill's philosophy is rooted in the concepts of maintaining a positive mental attitude and focusing on your vision. Visualization is a philosophy that has sustained my ability to make ideas, dreams, and hunches a reality. This concept and my faith in it is a private secret that I have rarely shared with anyone except intimate friends. If you can clearly see it and believe it, you can achieve it. This philosophy works if you are ready for it. It is habit forming and contagious. A Positive Mental Attitude held me together.

Amira's Birth

My wife Aleyah gave birth to our daughter Amira on January 31, 1992. At the age of 41, I began to grow weary of the Joe Clark routine. I was depleted of energy, fighting for my professional reputation and overworked. I had no life, but work. I was tired. My dedication to JHS 265 had over taken my life. My concern for Aleyah, Amira, personal ambition and survival instincts kept me going. Vividly, I remember Amira's birth. The doctors and midwife kept coaching Aleyah. I saw her pain and the strain of childbirth. It created sweat, foreign smells, matted hair of a mother and child engaged in a divine process guided by natural laws that no man can experience except as an outside observer.

The milky fluids seeped out of a clean shaven vagina and a small, wet, slimy head slowly slid into the gifted hands of a doctor waiting for my much loved love child to emerge. Mistakenly, I thought the umbilical cord was an elongated penis and I yelled, "A boy!" Proud, but sheepishly embarrassed, I was handed a daughter who instantaneously changed my life. Then, I sadly contemplated the kids at JHS 265. The overwhelming majority was on welfare. Most were being raised by a single mother. Few named a daddy as the head of a household. Then I became depressed and thought of all the little things I wished my father had done. The baseball games, Christmas, visiting school, taking me to church, fishing, hunting, riding the bicycle, and regularly buying food, clothes became seemingly supernatural events that I was never able to experience with my father. Amira was so tiny. She was beautiful! I was renewed and determined to continue in my profession as a principal!

I pondered and could not reconcile my understanding of history. Did slavery destroy the hearts, souls and spirits of Black men? Why are we so reluctant to publicly acknowledge and unconditionally love our children? Is it fear of failure? Prejudice and biases have damn near psychologically ruined us forever? Black men are imploding! My America, my God, can't you see what's happening to Black men?

Leaving New York

My number one goal during the 1995-96 school year was to leave New York City and the school alive. Threats, fights, crime in New York and the death of young people in the city, motivated me to focus on my life expectancy. One night, my wife overheard me talking about removing a cocked, loaded, automatic, 45-caliber gun from an angry, frustrated and irrational student. She cried, "I don't want to raise my children alone. You are not Superman! I do not want to go to your funeral and listen to hypocrites talk about how good a principal you were." I had nothing else to prove. I had proven that an effective principal could turn one of the most violent schools in New York City into a safe and orderly environment conducive to teaching and learning.

In 1996, I applied for the position of principal at my alma mater in Laurinburg, North Carolina. In the final phase of the selection process, Scotland County superintendent Dr. John Batchelor flew to New York, spent two days at JHS 265, and offered me the position at Scotland High School. I was going home. I was principal of JHS 265 for four years. Although I was leaving the city, for almost twenty years I had refused to stand on the sidelines Standing in the Shadows of Greatness.

The process of moving forces you to put your life in cardboard boxes. Driving South on Interstate 95 gave me 13 hours to reflect on the years I spent in the Big Apple. I had left home for college in June of 1970. I never dreamed of being a teacher or a principal. My teaching career started at Benjamin Franklin High School on November 11, 1978. I worked at Charles Evans Hughes, Boys and Girls, Tilden, and eventually, Dr. Susan S. McKinley JHS 265. While in New York City, I worked as an office temp for over 50 companies. I also earned a living as a landlord, karate teacher, actor, comedian, impressionist, writer, college professor, English teacher, assistant principal, and principal. The reflections of highs and lows often merged together. Contrasts were immeasurably thin. The criticism, vicious attacks, burglaries, broken windshields, slashed car tires, unemployment, eviction notices, accolades, applause, awards, dinners in my honor, testimonials, television, newspapers and speaking engagements created a headache and tears that blurred my vision.

December 17, 1992 my wife Aleyah rushed into my office with tears and sweat running down her face. The radio stations had reported that a popular Brooklyn principal had been killed coming to the aid of a student.

It was not me, but I had a very difficult time getting her to settle down. Patrick Francis Daly, principal of PS 15 in the Red Hook section of Brooklyn, was killed in the line of duty. For the first time, I questioned my ability to survive and effectively manage a school in New York City. There is no pity in the naked city. You do what you have to do. That's just the way it is!

Thousands of my students have graduated and moved on to the minefields of a world where only the strong survive. A few have become multimillionaires in entertainment and sports. The innocent holds a special place. Time is not kind enough to answer the ultimate question. Was it worth it? Did I make a difference? What happened to my aspirations to be an actor and writer? What happens now?

Forbidden Sex

Of the thousands of memories, an incident at JHS 265 made an encore on center stage in my mind. McKinney's young, innocent and vulnerable middle school students often broke my heart of hearts. As a trained thespian, I often walked through the school's theatre after hours. Perhaps it was an effort to exorcise demons and public solitude deeply embedded in my conscience. The theatre is a hollow sanctuary where actors retreat to reconnect with their inner souls. It remains an unfilled vessel of creativity and divine inspiration. This day, the mysterious shadows behind the stage emitted sounds reminiscent of a wounded animal during road kill. The deep panting breaths were overshadowed by the voice of a clumsy adolescent encouraging his willing but inexperienced partner in "the slow dance of forbidden passion" often depicted on cheap x-rated movies. The stars were a 15-year old young man and a 13-year old ingénue.

Perhaps her down payment will secure his monogamous affection until a safer time and place not interrupted by this uninvited "principle" disrupting this magic momentous escape from the tragic flaws of the ghetto. Her love was more important than any perfunctory punitive actions the chief executive officer could give. Now aware of an uninvited guest, her lover flees, knowing that she will forever protect his identity. If one of 10 million sperms makes it home, she will also relieve him of any responsibilities. That's the real deal in the city. If you play with fire, you get burned. You give it up or somebody else will. You got to give some to get some. I get mine and you get yours. Punishment, threats, and calls to her mother did not compel her to violate his trust. She refused to give his name. Unfortunately, this scene is repeated daily in schools, basements, closets, abandoned subway cars, on roofs, in cars, bedrooms, staircases, abandoned buildings, etc. Why? Because it feels good. Everyone else is doing it! Approximately 500,000 teenagers get pregnant each year. The lyrics of rock and roll, rhythm and blues, pop and rap music will echo cycles of this tragic and ritualistic rite of passage.

You Can't Go Home Again?

As we crossed the Scotland County line, the sight of Scotland High School rekindled high school memories. Ms. Nelson taught me journalism and was my inspiration as a writer. Ms. Buie was a masterful English teacher and linguistic technician. A secret crush on my drama teacher, Ms. Narramore, propelled me to the N. C. School of the Arts and rescued me from tobacco, cotton, the mills and factories. Mary Helen Speller and Madeo Hogue were tireless civil rights activists. However, Spencer Willard, my white Economics and U. S. History teacher, pierced through my inferiorities and bullshit. He challenged me to make something out of my life or be just another smart-ass with a big mouth. Willard was enthralled and shocked that I read everything that I could get my hands on. I also committed the unforgivable sin of challenging racial norms, economic theories, history and the power structure. Willard was articulate and held firm to his beliefs. Little did either of us know that his convictions and stubbornness would influence me for the rest of my life.

The superiority of the white Anglo-Saxon power structure was not acceptable to me when I was 16 years old. This resistance to established norms and mores intensified throughout my adulthood. Ironically, beliefs solidified at Scotland High School from 1968 to 1970 would come back to haunt me 25 years later.

Sallye McLaurin, my science teacher, was still there, still one of the prettiest and best-dressed girls in town. Sallye has always been a "fox." She often disciplined young men by hitting us in the head with the nearest object. We giggled and squirmed in our seats. Gosh, we all loved her. Sallye made it clear that she would always "beat some sense into my head." She said, "I'll get out of jail before you get out of the hospital!" Lillie Barber was the matriarch of teachers from the old days. Ms. Barber taught my mother at the one room Allen Chapel School in Pankey Town! She is especially loyal to kids from the all Black Carver High School. Carver is fondly remembered as our "colored" school that taught manners, character, obedience, pride, dignity, self respect and the Bible.

After integration, Black kids from Carver, Shaw, and I. E. Johnson were thrown together with white kids from Laurel Hill, Wagram and Laurinburg High School. Scotland High School became the new comprehensive high school dominated by the all-white culture of Laurinburg High School's "Fighting Scots." Despite very long bus rides, resistance, race riots and overt racism, Scotland's Fighting Scots became a permanent fixture of the county's culture. Unfortunately, nothing from the historical Black high schools was preserved. Our African ancestors were shipped to a strange land and left their history on the shores of the Nile. We were bused to a hostile and foreign environment and brought our history encased in our minds and hearts. The history and culture of the Black schools were never mentioned while I was a student at SHS. Blacks could only talk about the "good ole days." Although very little had changed, on July 2, 1996, I became Scotland High School's first African American principal.

The Laurinburg Exchange printed its headlines, "Pankey New SHS Principal." The subtitle added, "He Once Dreamed of Broadway." Destiny, Providence and Coincidence have blessed me with hundreds of cherished memories, rewards and opportunities. I was returning to Scotland High School as its first African American principal. Aleyah, Ashia, Amira and our dog, Kiki, arrived at our new home in the uncharted waters of the New South. Several Black churches welcomed my return and went into prayer for my safety and success. Why? I was unaware that the "scuttlebutt" rumor had spread that my wife was white. I assumed that Laurinburg had changed with the rest of the country. Little did I know of the 20th century high tech landmines waiting for me! I was happy to be home.

Coincidental with my arrival in Laurinburg, during the hot humid summer of 1996, the Laurinburg Exchange appointed a newcomer as editor of the town's sole newspaper. The local shock jock announcer and owner of a radio station began reporting many incidents that undermined my leadership at Scotland High School. On a statewide level, the hotly contested and racially divisive senatorial campaigns of white conservative Jesse Helms and Black moderate Harvey Gantt were explosive headlines in newspapers. It had been over 20 years since racial issues had hit me in the face. Ironically, the race riots at Scotland High School 25 years ago were my last encounter with race in your face. Racism is subtle in big cities.

The newspaper's editor wrote scathing anti-Pankey editorials and a local disc jockey's impersonation of Howard Stern were synonymous with national attacks of Black leaders throughout the country. Their tag team created a hostile environment for me. However, a large number of letters to the editor supported me. In the interest of political correctness and a desire to maintain their jobs and social status, a few residents swore race had nothing to do with anything. Privately, Aleyah and I could rarely get folks to talk about anything but race.

Prior to the opening of school in August, the newspaper published a story complete with a Black male's pants half way down his legs, showing off his underwear complete with a headline, "High School Students Don't Like Dress Code." The subtitle included a reference to rules banning sagging pants and short mini-skirts. The story created fear and generated debates before I was afforded an opportunity to meet with my students. Students constantly approached me at businesses and churches. They consistently asked me about uniforms, a bat, bullhorn, and putting people in jail.

The newspaper's derogatory photograph was offensive to the Black community and created animosity among various ethnic groups. "A mean, bat wielding, bullhorn toting, loud, angry know-it-all Black radical had been appointed principal." Fear of change gripped the neighborhoods. The radio disc jockey used other people's anxiety to increase his status and popularity as the exclusive person "in the know" and the fighter for the community's best interest. Black folks were hurt, frightened and incensed. Black senior citizens from the segregated Civil Rights era routinely hugged me and wept for joy during my first speaking engagement at Bright Hopewell Baptist Church. The Reverend Garland Pierce stated that he had waited a long time to hear "such a speech." Church members welcomed the new rules that included wearing pants above the waist, no beepers, no cell phones, skirts above the knees, no skin tight spandex butt gripping tights, lined paper, hard notebooks, paper, pencil, the return of manners and The Pledge of Allegiance.

Black folks had not seen these rules and regulations since the closings of the "colored" schools. They were aware that drugs and teen pregnancy had a grip on Black neighborhoods. Black kids needed a leader and role model empowered to implement policies designed to teach marketable skills and discipline.

Several respected African American leaders advised me to imagine going back 20 years in time. They cautioned me that the South was still the South. I listened in disbelief when a radio host made jokes about the new rules based on effective schools research. He got a hoot about the new rule requiring students to read books. Despite being one of the most awarded and respected school principals in the country, he was slamming me on the radio. Thus, to get my real message to the community, I accepted close to 50 speaking engagements during my first year. In retrospect, although, it didn't always seem like it at the time, the overwhelming majority of the community was supportive and hopeful about a student-centered vision. Business, religious and civic organizations applauded the efforts of the administration and staff.

Scotland High School is the home of the Fighting Scots. It is the hub of the community and the source of emotionally laden zealous pride. However, my analysis of the school's profile revealed thousands of discipline referrals in one year. School fights, a 30-point drop on S. A. T. scores, low test scores, an unacceptable dropout rate, and a high number of teen pregnancies were challenges that required focused attention. The problems were no different from those in most American cities. The overall talent, dedication and commitment of teachers were superior to anything I had witnessed in my lifetime. Actually the school was ready to move forward, but far too many self-appointed principals and education leaders wanted to return the school to the good ole days. The analysis of the data indicated it was time for a change. Denial and racially divisive commentaries could not help our school. The school is a diamond in the midst of the community. We needed to make a good school better. The school was Standing in the Shadows of Greatness.

Football is a sacred untouchable God in Scotland County and throughout the South. The closest thing to heaven is beating Richmond County High School. During football season, the county comes to a standstill on Friday nights.

Part of the radio announcer's popularity is his devout and fanatical support of SHS's football program. A large portion of his radio airtime is dedicated to publicizing and debating football, sports, and other activities at the school. The local newspaper is equally supportive. There is a vast difference between reporting the news and education expertise. Although the public does have a right to voice opinions, all opinions are not created equal.

The Dawn Of A New Era

Reportedly, football provided an outlet for athletes, and games afforded town residents the opportunity to gather together. Teenagers could chat and visit with coeds, relax and enjoy the social amenities traditionally associated with small town sporting events. My advisors informed me that Friday night games were innocent small town "laid-back gatherings" to "chew the fat." Game time is 7:30 p.m. Go Scots go!

Yankee Stadium, Madison Square Garden and the Meadowlands regularly plays host to over 45-50,000 fans, but I had never witnessed the chaos and confusion experienced at Scotland's first home game. Most of the guests were well behaved. Small gangs of unsupervised teens, blatantly, and without fear of repercussions, knocked people out of the way or intimidated them with mini posses composed of neighborhood wannabe bullies wearing scarves and earrings. Approximately 10 Black teenagers chased two elementary school white boys and threatened to beat the "living hell" out of them for no apparent reason. The smell of marijuana circulated under the bleachers and near the fences where the neighborhood dealers were conducting business. We had one or two fights. Church-going senior citizens got an earful of profanity. We won the game. Cheerleaders brought the house down. The Scotland High School Marching Band is one of the best bands in the state. They were sensational! Most folks left the stadium by 10.00 pm. As late as 1:00 a. m., I was taking abandoned students home. And a good time was had by all.

Controversial New Rules

Monday, an emergency meeting of administrators was called and I expressed my disappointment that misinformation was given to me. Will somebody please tell me what I saw was my imagination? What relaxed atmosphere? Did I see drug deals? Did I hear profanity? Was those real fights or wrestle mania?

Effective immediately, new rules governing game decorum were mandated. Metal detectors were to be used and spectators were required to sit during the game. Reasonable movement that involved bathroom visits and concession stands was allowed. Standing in the front of fences, blocking spectators, cursing, swearing, drugs, heavy petting, threats, intimidation, alcohol, and smoking were outlawed. We also wanted everyone to stand for the Star Spangled Banner.

The local media denounced the new rules. Allegedly, spectators never saw the transgressions. Predictable letters to the editor and calls to the radio station added fuel to the debate. One writer to the newspaper compared me to Hitler and declared no one would attend games. The good news was that many letters consistently supported the new rules and regulations. The truth is attendance at games hinged on the quality of the football team and the rivalry between our opponents and us. Senior citizens thanked me for restoring a wholesome family environment. Letters for and against the rules were published in the local newspaper. Radio commentary was against the new rules. (In August 2003, seven years later, similar rules were published in the local newspaper.)

Other changes resulted from numerous meetings with students, administrative planning strategies, and faculty conferences. Press conferences and town meetings were called to discuss the research and experience-based reasons for making dramatic changes in the school culture. Although, I am a Laurinburg native, I could not ignore the knowledge learned during 18 years of experience in the New York school system.

A few fans from Richmond Senior High School refused to take off their hats and stand for the National Anthem. I returned their money and had the police escort them off the premises. They were aware that I was scheduled to be the keynote speaker at their school. They threatened me and told me I better not show up for the engagement. Laurinburg Police Officer Keith Johnson drove me to the event. The Richmond County Sheriff Department met me at the county line and gave me a law enforcement escort. They escorted me into the city, stayed with me and escorted me back to Scotland County.

The SHS culture had ignored sagging pants and other values popularized by gangsta rappers and urban gang bangers. Sagging pants are popular in jails, because prisoners cannot wear belts. Dropping your pants and showing underwear or flesh is an invaluable advertising technique used by the homosexual prison population. Shoestrings are not allowed in some jails, because prisoners use them to strangle inmates or themselves. The wearing of big clothes is the quintessential trademark of urban street punks for "packing" or the concealment of weapons. Duke University, University of North Carolina in Chapel Hill, Indiana, UCLA, Kansas, Connecticut and other highly successful university basketball teams' attire have become the favorite clothing of big city gangs. Although, the South has opted for denial, gangs are alive, doing well and growing in popularity. "Ignore" is the root of ignorance. The wearing of big rings is used as a substitute for brass knuckles. The principal's principles should be the moral and ethical conscience of the school. However, morality-based on perfection often leads to hypocrisy and cynicism. State, federal laws and Supreme Court rulings give school officials the authority to mandate discipline and dress codes that are morally sound and in the best interest of children. I was appointed the principal of Scotland High School. I could not allow public opinion, fads or whims deny students a safe and orderly environment designed to enhance student achievement. In hindsight, I should have consulted with teachers and parents before the implementation of some of the new rules. I was wrong to act without consultation. I was stubborn and I paid a price. "Principles are more important than being principal." I knew in my heart of hearts that I was Standing in the Shadows of Greatness.

The Price Of Being A Change Agent

Despite ongoing controversies and resistance, it appeared that the majority of the county supported my policies. There were times when the radio station called me within two minutes of my morning announcements. Someone from the school was leaking or misrepresenting my daily announcements, policies, and faculty conference agendas. The station's owner invited me to co-host a radio show and offered a rebuttal to critics. I refused. My only agenda was the improvement of SHS.

Something exhilarating was happening in the Black churches. Some Sundays I had two speaking engagements. One Sunday I spoke at three different churches. For the record, I had many speaking engagements at white churches, too. They were very responsive and supportive. Worshippers testified, cried, shouted encouragement and gave me the courage to "keep the faith." The Black church was the bully pulpit of my forefathers. I needed the church. It was my best voice of effective communication. The church is the religious and power base of the community. Even winos got enough sense to go to church. None of us is crazy enough to ignore our religious upbringing.

African Americans left the South in the 1950's-70's. Black baby boomers are highly educated. They are coming home. They have good incomes. They are not afraid. They don't have the fear and intimidation attributed to Black Southerners who stayed home. I represent a small Black dewdrop of a migrating flood headed South. My arrival signals the increasing influx of returning African Americans that will challenge old racial norms, stereotypes, arrogance, the color complex, and the Confederate Flag. We come in peace. "Ain't nothing gonna turn us around! We are on the move, now. Like an idea whose time has come!"

The principal is the chief executive officer of the school. Perhaps, I disappointed those interested in a ceremonial figurehead. Deliberate efforts were made to work with community based organizations, school officials and the staff. However, the student editor of the school newspaper joined the anti-Pankey group. The "Bagpipe" published an article that stated I had "removed the stalls from the boys' bathroom and was treating students like barnyard animals." The article was read over the airwaves on the local radio station. This despicable act should have been beneath responsible adults, because the stalls were removed when I was a student at the school in 1970. Everyone knew it. Yet, the newspaper advisor and owner of the radio station allowed this information to reach the public.

The Courage To Lead

Many members faculty were highly skilled, dedicated, highly professional, supportive, and conducted themselves with dignity. Disagreement does not mean disloyalty. If all of us think alike, somebody is not thinking. Without hesitation, I publicly declare that I am forever indebted to them. Very few file-letters were written for insubordination and conduct unbecoming teachers. Teachers willingly followed the North Carolina Department of Instruction's Standard Course of Study. The assistant principals and department leaders took the necessary steps to insure that the Best Practices developed by the North Carolina Department of Public Instruction were followed. These guidelines called the Teacher Performance Appraisal Instrument have proven to consistently improve student achievement. The Best Practices teaching strategies of TPAI are summarized below:

Instructional time:
Materials ready
Class started on time
Gets students on task
Maintains high level of engagement-time on task

Student Behavior:
Rules are in place and followed
Verbal comments are respectful
Movement is appropriate
The teacher monitors behavior
Stops inappropriate behavior
Instructional Presentation:
Review

Introduces lesson:
Speaks fluently
Lesson understandable
Provides relevant examples
Success demonstrated on tasks
Appropriate level of questions
Brisk pace
Efficient & smooth transitions
Assignments are clear
Summarizes main points

Instructional Monitoring:
Maintains strict standards & adherence to deadlines
Check student performance
Work products to check progress
Questions clearly and one at a time

Instructional Feedback:
Immediate In class feedback
Feedback given on homework
Sustained feedback

Facilitating Instruction:
Instruction aligned with the state's curriculum
Using diagnostic information and assessment to improve
      instruction
Maintains accurate records
Additional resources used to improve student achievement

Communicating In the Educational Environment:
Treat all students fairly
Participates in development of the school's vision
Good relationships

Performing Non-Instructional Duties:
Willing carries out non-instructional duties
Lifelong learners
Reflective practitioner

They consistently taught from well-developed lesson plans. The curriculum was aligned with state-mandated tests. Benchmark tests indicated student achievement was on the upswing and teachers volunteered as tutors a countless number of hours. New procedures were in place to establish a research-based school improvement plan and standard operating procedures. Teachers worked very hard.

It was never about me. Principals must have the courage to make decisions that are good for children. The malcontents sent my memos and their versions of directives to the superintendent, school board, newspapers and radio station. Despite the unswerving support of the superintendent, we spent excessive energy clarifying policies and engaging in damage control. However, I never backed away from research and experience-based effective schools best practices. A respected central office official advised me that I was already a successful principal when I came to Laurinburg. Gossip inflicted the most painful wounds.

From 100 to 700 students supported Dress for Success on different days. Some days they exceeded my expectations and on other days I was disappointed. Dress for Success was 100% voluntary. It was an awesome sight seeing students dressed up on Tuesdays and Thursdays. Our Dress for Success coordinator, Mike Fedak was able to get local businessmen to donate money, televisions, CD players, and 25 laptop computers to the Dress for Success program. Although The Laurinburg Exchange ran an editorial stating that Dress For Success was dividing the community, it published my rebuttal. I reminded readers that Dress for Success was endorsed by major newspapers such as the highly respected New York Times. The program also received accolades from WABC, WCBS, WNBC, corporate

America, community-based organizations and the churches. Letters pro and con were printed in the school and local newspapers. School board member Dr. William Morgan wrote a strong letter of support. The Black community wanted their children to Dress for Success.

Dress for Success was an answer to young men wearing their pants low enough to show their naked butts. Pants were worn low enough that when the wind blew the butts would whistle. A lot of folks complained about rap music, but a lot of the noise was not rap music, but butts whistling in the wind. Folks were tired of the out of control dress code adopted by teenagers. Girls wore Daisy Duke short pants and skirts were often so short that they had frostbitten thighs. Girls would bend over and little boys could see as far away as Alaska. Boys wore their pants way down and girls wore their skirts very short and Scotland County had one of the highest teen pregnancy rates in the state. And you wonder why there are so many illegitimate babies? When students show their underwear and naked butts, it's time for adults to stand up and say enough is enough. Advertisers and celebrities exploit children as they sell clothes and make money. Children are not mature enough to dictate the moral compass of a community. My consistent message to adults was "Take Back Your Schools. Take Back The Hearts, Souls And Minds of Our Children." Ricki Lake, Jerry Springer, Mike Tyson, Dennis Rodman, vulgar celebrities, x-rated rappers, half naked butt-grinding sexually suggestive video artists, and gross comedians are too slimy and degenerate to set the moral tone for young people.

While some adults are stuck in denial, Jerry Springer has emerged as the number one teacher of sex education and morality for our babies. Enough is enough! Principles are more important than being principal. Why should we forever find ourselves Standing in the Shadows of Greatness?

The Sermon You Live

The sermon you live is much more powerful than the one you preach.

The Black preachers designed sermons supporting Dress for Success and other policies that would restore cleanliness and morality in the community. The Black church was a Rock of Gibraltar and staunch supporter. Historically, Black segregated schools inspected students and enforced very rigid discipline and dress codes. Eyes, nappy heads, ears, teeth, shirt collars, fingernails, wrinkled clothes, shoes and notebooks were routinely inspected. In the "Good Ole Days," reprimands, chastisements and whippings with a switch or belt were in order if you dared to fail an inspection. Dress for Success reminded Black folks of the days before desegregation.

The old folks preached: Before desegregation "chillun" listened to their elders. Integration ruined colored folks! That new man at the school is teaching them little rotten rascals to have manners and say "good morning," "good afternoon," "please", "may I," and "thank you." They oughta say, "Yes sir," and "no ma'am" or they should feel welts on their backsides. We should bring back the switch, belts and razor straps. And if the switch is too small, they oughta beat'em with it and get another one. Two beatings better than one. The man writing the newspaper don't know what he talkin' about. Integration damn near ruint Black chilluns-specially boys. Leave him alone and let'im do his job. Give me my spit cup. Sides, gotta dip my snuff.

Listen to the old timers. Don't be too quick to censure poor folks. They may not have money or power, but they can keep us from losing our souls.

The Best Of Times & The Worst Of Times

We made a good school better. Our test scores improved. Despite ongoing ethnic tension, we put in place Effective Schools standard operating procedures, strict discipline, metal detectors, and surveillance cameras. The dropout rate went down 25%, violence was reduced dramatically, and the number of discipline referrals was substantially eliminated. In addition our S. A. T. scores increased by 17 points. Every criteria used by the North Carolina Department of Public Instruction indicated a major improvement. The data proved beyond a doubt that the overwhelming majority of our educators were effective teachers.

Rivalry and hostility between groups of Black boys created a need for intense peer mediation the last week of school. Despite my instincts, I did not suspend the two opposing groups. Safety Resource Officer Keith Johnson, Assistant Principal Kenneth Harrell, and I engaged in marathon negotiations in an effort to avoid an impending fight. Although, both parties agreed to a truce, they violated their promise, and fought the last day of school. The radio station blasted, "Principal Henry Pankey's hope for a nonviolent school year came to an end when 11 students were involved in a fight the last day of school." Despite having one of the safest years in the school's history, the newspaper also wrote headlines and published letters about the fight. One letter stated this was the worse fight to ever happen at SHS. Conveniently, they forgot the race riots of the 60's and 70's.

Folks were quick to remind everyone that earlier in the year I had mistakenly stated that we had not had a fight in two months. (They researched and discovered one fight.) Staff members were quick to call board members and call me a liar. However, the year before my arrival, two students were shot on campus and 262 fights or "incidents" were recorded in the school's discipline report. In addition hundreds of students were involved in fights during the riots of the 60's and 70's. We logged a total of approximately 29 fights. Yet, one fight

97

was magnified as a major failure of my administration. Yes, 11 students were involved in the fight, but we had significantly eliminated discipline referrals and fights.

My graduation speech a few days later added more fuel to the fire. During the speech I told the class of 1997 that they were the most outstanding class in the history of Scotland High School second to none. I received enthusiastic applause, shouts, testifying and a standing ovation after the presentation. The newspapers and radio station called it the most controversial speech in the history of the school. It was played on the radio for approximately a week. Listeners called to voice their disapproval of my speaking style and its content. The hometown newspaper ran letters to the editor supporting and denouncing the speech for three weeks. Some critics contended that I had sent the audience into a frenzy. Others were upset that I sounded like an African American minister. The Black community was inspired by the speech and hurt by the criticism. Some compared it to Dr. Martin Luther King's "I Have a Dream" speech. Many whites supported the speech, my policies and my administration.

Leadership is not about theatrics. It is about vision, courage, risk-taking, providing inspiration and holding steadfast to noble principles. Too often leaders use consensus as a mask for the lack of courage. As summarized in this anonymous poem, leaders often take risks despite criticism:

In the battle of life, it is not the critic who counts; nor the one who points out how the strong person stumbled, or where the doer of a deed could have done better. The credit belongs to the person who is actually in the arena; whose face is marred by dust and sweat and blood, who strives valiantly, who errs and comes short again and again, because there is no effort without error and shortcoming; who does actually strive to do deeds; who knows the great enthusiasm, the great devotion, spends oneself in a worthy cause; who at best knows in the end the triumph of high achievement, and who at worst, if he or she fails, at least fails while daring greatly. Far better it is to dare mighty things, to win glorious triumphs even though checkered by failure, than to rank with those timid spirits who neither enjoy nor suffer much because they live in the gray twilight that knows neither victory nor defeat.

Scotland High School's test scores rose substantially, but the story was the smallest written about me during the entire time I was at the school. Very little was said about the decreased dropout rate. This is significant because there is only one high school in the entire county, but the good news was not publicized. The next year's opening was successful and the reduction in violence was a one liner buried in another article.

By now, Aleyah was lethargic and tired. The kids were fine. I began to question my value as principal. My job was to improve the school. Rumors are one of the prices you pay for being high profile. You become the hottest news in town. The truth was rarely allowed to interfere with lies. One Black elected official told me that I was an outsider. He is also the same member of the city council responsible for spreading the rumor that I had a white wife. Although I was raised in Laurinburg, I wasn't considered from being "around here anymore." You can't go home again? Yes, you can. Many people strongly supported my vision for the school. Superintendent Dr. John Batchelor, Deputy Superintendent Norwood Randolph, the Scotland County Board Of Education, John Speller, Wilbert Riggins, Joyce Riggins, businessman Walter Lee Rogers, Police Chief Robert Malloy, member of the N. C. house of representatives Doug Yongue, retired educator Lillie Barber, teacher Sallye McLaurin, central office administrators Linda Douglas and Annie Cureton's vision, integrity, loyalty represent the type of stakeholders' vindication that all leaders need in order to be successful.

Brian, and Alicia Krout, Jim and Marsha Siedliski developed an important network that gave my family additional support needed during very difficult times. Linda Covington, Carmen Hicks, David Stone, J. D. Willis, Shep Jones, Stacy Stewart, Charles McDuffie and Robert Brown gave me the courage and guidance to stay true to my beliefs. They consistently reminded me to heed Shakespeare's advice, "To thine own self be true." My aunt Clara McNeil's children helped me tremendously. Perhaps nobody was as important to me as Laurinburg's Police Chief Robert Malloy.

Chief Malloy is African-American. He is brilliant, but his exceptional interpersonal communication skills have greatly enhanced his ability to survive a 30-year career in the police department. Aleyah has been great throughout our marriage.

Very few men are successful without the support of a dedicated wife. The leader and spouse are partners. Aleyah's parents, Raymond and Doris Pryor, raised an extraordinary young lady. Aleyah and I are forever indebted to the Laurinburg community for helping us create and implement a shared vision. Leaders cannot be successful without leaders of leaders championing the vision.

Ironically, I was a Southerner in New York, but I also felt like an outsider in my hometown. The role of principal includes many hours of reflective solitude. George Bernard Shaw once said, "Fatigue makes cowards of us all." It also makes us weary, but we would be wise to accentuate the positive:

Praise...
He's a good role model.
Test scores improved.
The dropout rate went down.
He's an excellent orator.

"He has an outstanding record behind him, so let us all give him a chance to weave his magic."
 – Bill Morgan, Scotland County School Board Member

"Pankey returned to his alma mater in 1996 as Scotland High's principal. He struggled, despite controversy and criticism, to achieve the North Carolina Department of Public Instruction Exemplary Status and to claim the Safe School Award..." – Laurinburg Exchange, March 1, 2000

"As the new principal of Scotland High School, the school's safety record is perhaps the best in the Tarheel state."
 – Administrative Weekly Digest, November 18, 1996

"SAT scores up in 1997 For Scotland High Students"
"Scores on End of Course tests rose at Scotland High School in 1996-97" – Laurinburg Exchange Headlines August 28, 1997

"One of the things this school system needs is discipline, and that is one of the changes Principal Henry Pankey has been charged to implement." – Joseph J. Bennett

"Mr. Pankey did an incredible job of encouraging us and making us feel one in a million. He told us we were magnificent and the most outstanding class at Scotland High School."

– LeShondra McCrimmon

"It is great for me to have someone help me make better decisions about my life and how to become a better student, person and individual."   – Damon Leach

Albert Einstein stated, "Great spirits have always encountered violent opposition from mediocre minds." Rumors that lead to poisonous character assassination are the most potent weapon used against change agents. Supporters of the status quo are often rewarded. Change advocates are usually beaten into submission. It may appear to be racial, but it is bigger than race. It's bigger than me and it's bigger than Scotland County. It is normal human behavior to resist change. The nature of a thing in existence is to continue to exist in its present form. "It is because it resists change that we say pride goeth before the fall." Most systems support the status quo.

Martin Luther King, Jr. once stated. "Evil triumphant is somehow weaker than right defeated." Machiavelli succinctly describes the plight of principals with principles. "There is nothing more difficult to manage, more dubious to accomplish, nor more doubtful of success than to initiate a new order of things. The reformer has enemies in all those who profit from the old order and only lukewarm defenders in all those who would profit from the new order." America is still struggling with 400 years of unresolved racial problems. Change is more potent than racism. Fear cannot stop change. The invention and use of computers will leave ignorant people in the age of the portable typewriter and mule wagon. Change will come in megabytes.

The given circumstances were not fair to a devoted wife from a city of eight million people, Macy's, Bloomingdales, Broadway, professional entertainment, Wall Street, and the shopping capital of the world. Wal-Mart wasn't cutting it anymore. Relaxation is fine but, at some point, urbanites need stimulation. Job offers were coming in and I had to make some serious decisions about my health, marriage, reputation and career. For almost 20 years, I had meticulously worked toward the development of a national reputation. Was I willing to give it all up? The radio station and newspapers were not going to let up. The level of school improvement was exemplary by the standards, norms and criteria developed by national school improvement experts, but some in the community were not ready to accept this change agent.

Scotland County's superintendent Dr. John Batchelor and I first discussed my future when he visited me in New York during my initial interview for the job. His progressive vision of education impressed me. His courage or craziness was first shown when he offered to walk through the Fort Green projects to New York's subway system. Candidly, I told him that the muggers would probably kill each other fighting over who would rob the super crazy or super rich white man walking through the ghetto. In hindsight, Batchelor would have made it! My respect and admiration for him remained strong throughout my trials and triumphs. His loyalty and support made it difficult for me to tell him that I had accepted the job as principal of Southern Durham High School. We were both pleased to note that the N. C. Dept. Of Public Instruction recognized Scotland High School as a "Safe School" and the school also received "Exemplary Status." His leadership was undeniable when every school in Scotland County received Exemplary Status.

Thank God, I had not let down the people who had confidence in me. The pride of the African American community means a lot to me. I am so thankful that the school was recognized by the state. They also needed a principal with courage and convictions. I walked into Scotland High School with my head up and walked out standing taller. It is easy to stand tall when you are standing on someone else's shoulders. I am forever indebted to the students, staff and Scotland County community. Overall, the School Board was a staunch ally. My assistant principals were loyal, competent and focused on the success of the school:

Emma McNeill	Leonard Huffman
Mike Cafaro	Denise Jennings
Ken Harrell	Jean Phifer
Dr. Wayne Scott	Dr. Barry Wall
Steve Hagen	Willie Thomas

The people of Scotland County gave me strong shoulders to stand on. Criticism is the bitter medicine that forces leaders to reflect and mature. If I could live my life all over again, I would ask God to allow me the opportunity to relive the two years I was principal of Scotland High School.

Taking the Helm Of A Low Performing School

Prior to my appointment, Southern Durham High School was identified by the state of North Carolina as one of 11 low performing schools. The school had a history of discipline problems, violence, racism, high teacher turnover and poor student achievement. Before school started, I sent out a blue sheet outlining my vision, high expectations, a new dress and discipline policies. The Raleigh News and Observer and the Durham Herald Sun praised me as a nationally acclaimed educator and "tough love" principal. The press in the Raleigh, Durham and Chapel Hill triangle is directly aligned with the national effective school movement. They also supported the concept of a safe and orderly environment controlled by professional educators. The Research Triangle area is a progressive minded community with a superb concentration of universities, educated citizens, and rated as one of the best places to live in America. The parents, teachers, staff and Southern Durham community welcomed a "change agent."

Based on popular demand, we scheduled three meet the principal evening orientation sessions instead of the customary single meeting. The meetings were informative and exciting. Expectations were high and the Southern High School community was cautiously hopeful. My first task was to analyze the data and review the school improvement plan. The school improvement team and I had several meetings. There I shared my education philosophy and discussed research-based best practices. Collaboratively, our team modified the school improvement plan. Most school improvement plans are well written and Southern was no exception. However, school improvement plans are rarely read or followed. Improvement plans or goals are useless unless they are followed and include an ongoing assessment tool. We agreed to implement the plan. The pressure was on!

Standing in the Shadows of Greatness dominated my mind as I searched for words to comfort the staff of Southern High School. As one of 11 North Carolina high schools to receive a "Low Performing" rating, the staff, parents, students and community were demoralized. I was greeted with horror stories about fights, chaos, drug deals, low achieving students, and a tarnished reputation. The second eye was blackened with data indicating a decrease in S. A. T. scores. Poor student achievement had plagued the school since the city and county school merger in 1992. Expectations were low, morale had hit rock bottom, trembling voices, and fear and panic telegraphed that insurmountable obstacles had destined the school for failure. However, I felt the staff's pride, dedication and determination.

Also, I sensed a stronger acceptance of my education philosophy and leadership style than I had ever experienced in my life.

I gave out gold medals to every administrator, teacher, counselor, teacher's assistant, secretary, cafeteria worker, bus driver and janitor and declared that we were taking back our school, pride, dignity and self-respect. Southern High School was destined to be the new miracle of 800 Clayton Road as well as the pride and joy of Durham Public Schools. "From diamonds in the rough, we will create crown jewels!"

From A Diamond In The Rough To A Crown Jewel

The television stations and newspapers gave us incredible support and expressed confidence that the former actor and New York City principal was turning around Durham's only low performing high school. Speaking engagements, awards and honors followed the most remarkable school improvement transition that I have ever witnessed or read about. Within four months, test scores rocketed upward. The staff came together as a team destined to capture lightning in a bottle. We experienced resistance and difficulties that are normally associated with the culture of comprehensive high schools. Southern High School received certification as "A Safe School" and "Exemplary Status" for the 1998-99 school year. This recognition by the North Carolina Department of Public Instruction was covered by every major newspaper in the state. The test scores were published on websites in many newspapers.

Southern High School Update

In addition to the awards cited by DPI, we made progress with Dress for Success. Community based organizations, corporate America, religious institutions and many parents were pleasantly surprised that high school students would volunteer to dress up two days a week. It shocked and inspired all of Durham to see young men dressed in suits on their way to school. Many visiting students were against our dress code until they saw young ladies and young men dressed for success. Yes, students will complain about the dress code and then go out and spend hundreds of dollars to be part of a success story. We praised students for dressing up and gave away concert tickets, remote control color televisions sets, CD players, lap top computers, and cars. Yes, cars! Gifts were donated by individuals and corporations. We added another school program called Diamonds In The Rough. Diamonds In The Rough's goal was to raise a $1,000 scholarship for every SHS student who enrolls in a trade school, community or four-year college. We conducted a statewide fund raising campaign and raised several thousand dollars for Diamonds In The Rough.

SOUTHERN HIGH SCHOOL UPDATE
(January 19, 1999)

All of 97-98 vs. 1st Semester 98-99 (only)			
Course	97-98 Pct. Prof.	98-99 Pct. Prof.	Change Pct. Prof.
Algebra I	21.8%	36.3%	+14.5%
Algebra II	34.8%	41.4%	+6.6%
Biology	42.0%	54.8%	+12.8%
Chemistry	55.3%	66.6%	+11.3%
ELP	38.4%	48.1%	+9.7%
English I	39.7%	56.6%	+16.9%
English II	27.0%	52.6%	+25.6%
Geometry	30.5%	25.9%	-4.6%
Physics	50.0%	53.3%	+3.3%
Physical Sci	48.6%	58.3%	+9.7%
U. S. History	35.7%	35.3%	-0.4%

1st Semester 97-98 (only) vs. 1st Semester 98-99 (only)			
Course	97-98 Pct. Prof.	98-99 Pct. Prof.	Change Pct. Prof.
Algebra I	19.7%	36.3%	+16.6%
Algebra II	34.9%	41.4%	+6.5%
Biology	41.2%	54.8%	+13.6%
Chemistry	57.1%	66.6%	+9.5%
ELP	33.7%	48.1%	+14.4%
English I	47.1%	56.6%	+9.5%
English II	17.8%	52.6%	+34.8%
Geometry	16.1%	25.9%	+9.8%
Physics	57.6%	53.3%	-4.3%
Physical Sci	34.8%	58.3%	+23.5%
U. S. History	27.0%	35.3%	+8.3%

1st Semesters only: 96-97, 97-98, 98-99			
Course	97-98 Pct. Prof.	98-99 Pct. Prof.	98-99 Pct. Prof.	3-Yr Chg Pct. Prof.
Algebra I	17.3%	19.7%	36.3%	+19.0%
Algebra II	23.9%	34.9%	41.4%	+17.5%
Biology	40.6%	41.2%	54.8%	+14.2%
Chemistry	56.4%	57.1%	66.6%	+10.2%
ELP	37.5%	33.7%	48.1%	+10.6%
English I	44.6%	47.1%	56.6%	+12.0%
English II	26.8%	17.8%	52.6%	+25.8%
Geometry	8.6%	16.1%	25.9%	+17.3%
Physics	39.5%	57.6%	53.3%	+13.8%
Physical Sci	37.5%	34.8%	58.3%	+20.8%
U. S. History	44.8%	27.0%	35.3%	-9.5%

Although I issued directives that included the alignment of curriculum with standardized tests, these directives needed closer supervision. Best Practices require frequent monitoring of student achievement. This strategy can possibly eliminate surprises and predict student achievement before state examinations are administered. Even in low performing schools, teachers will resist positive changes and cling to old habits. The changing of rules or administrators does not institutionalize Best Practices. It is essential that school programs follow Best Practices with a successful track record. Tests are important, but we need to keep the focus on children.

Success is not a mystery. It is the result of good planning, hard work and belief in people. I've internalized the philosophy of David Hornbeck; "We know how to succeed with children from diverse circumstances. To succeed is not easy and, in some instances, it is extremely difficult. But the routes to success are not mysterious." We can unlock the mystery of school improvement if a school wants to improve and if school officials follow the formula. Do we have the commitment to do it? The status quo must go and we need to expand our comfort zones. Success is unchartered territory for many students and parents. To some students, school is the enemy. Are we content to forever find ourselves Standing in the Shadows of Greatness?

At Risk African American Children

Throughout my career, I've harbored grave and haunting concerns about the low achievement of African American students. Not surprisingly, expert educators and researchers are consistently baffled and mystified by the chronic low achievement of Blacks in this country. We need to be worried. Despite self-esteem classes, accountability mandates and spending billions of dollars, low student achievement is one of the most embarrassing challenges we face today. White educators secretly whisper about this trend, but they fear charges of racism. The majority of educators are white and female. Does this have an impact on Black student achievement? Blacks are quick to blame the invisible "they." Black educators are aware of the low achievement of Black students, but they don't want to be called "sellouts" or "Uncle Toms." Educators such as Joe Clark, James Comer, Lorraine Monroe, Jaime Escalante, Frank Mickens and others have experienced success improving the academic achievement of minority students. The common philosophy is the dire need to improve relationships. James Comer of the Yale School Development Program is right. "Nothing is more important to success in schools than the quality of relationships between and among students, staff and parents." The history, culture, norms, learning style, language and psychological development of minorities represent issues that professional educators are slow to explore in a non-patronizing, objective manner. Perhaps Thomas Jefferson was prophetic when he said, "I tremble for my country when I consider God is just, and his justice will not sleep forever."

My fear is that we will continue to pay dearly for our refusal to acknowledge the developmental needs of African American children. Low tests scores may represent a rebellion by Black students. Perhaps the scores represent passive civil disobedience. Why are so many brilliant Black students flunking basic competency exams? Are Black boys demonstrating to us that being actively involved (rap) is their best learning style? Are we too arrogant to pay attention to the cries of poor and minority children? They and our immigrants are not stupid. Why are their test scores so low? What is the best way to assess what they know and are able to do?

Black children need structure and the guidance of benevolent disciplinarians. They don't need pity or patronization. Stand in front of a school and you may see up to 50% of African American children attend school each day without a notebook, books, paper or pencil. Yet they will wear the most expensive designer clothes, latest hairstyles, fake gold jewelry, and $175.00 sneakers. They also have an unacceptable low academic achievement rate and comprise the majority of our suspensions or assignments to special education. At home, they spend from 40-60 hours in front of the television, video games and partying each week. They are most likely to engage in at risk behavior. About 30% of Black newborns are illegitimate. Until we organize the entire village, we will continue to play Russian roulette with the lives of our Black children.

"When the hut is burning, there is no time to argue." Making beds in a burning house is useless. "No problem can be solved from the same consciousness that created it." Our children need brave and unconditional tough love. They don't need posturing or opinion polls. They need a mama and a daddy. They need tough love and benevolent disciplinarians. The essence of tough love is to remedy failure and reward success.

Joe Clark, Frank Mickens and Henry Pankey have received brutal criticism for a no-nonsense approach that holds Blacks as well as the system equally accountable for the mis-education and lack of courage to discipline young people. Education malpractice must be stopped.

The 1998-99 school year at Southern High School was an extraordinary success. The Rotary, Ruritan, and Civitan organizations invited me to numerous speaking engagements. My audience slowly shifted from the traditional Black church and began to include the education establishment as well as moderate and conservative whites. The transition took me by surprise. The power brokers and average citizens want the same thing. They want safe and orderly schools composed of mannerly and high achieving students.

The killings at Columbine High School increased my support base. I am convinced Columbine saved my career. Now, people will listen to me. We were shocked as a nation. School safety has become the nation's number one public school priority. Despite the recent school killings and confiscation of nearly 6,000 guns a year, many school officials lack the courage to install metal detectors and video cameras. Character education programs usually involve posters and a motivational speaker. The courage to take back our schools and instill a moral compass guided by ethical values is still on the back burner. Politicians and status quo educators are concerned about appearances. Dead students do not do well on standardized tests and body bags are not good public relations props. The dropout rate, teen pregnancies, suspensions and body counts have increased the pressure to give the public safe and orderly schools of excellence or deal with the reality of vouchers and charter schools. Many status quo career educators are suffering from post-traumatic shock from the rash of blatant school killings. Wake up. Move forward. We owe it to our children to develop schools of excellence for all children. We must address the developmental needs of all children. If we don't act with vision and courage, career politicians will only give us symbolic postings of Biblical commandments, school uniforms and a military like security force in our schools. James Comer's plea for addressing the needs of the total child is a lone voice in the wilderness. Howard Garner's findings about multiple intelligence are ignored. My fear is that we will have erratic and politically expedient knee jerk reactions that are not well thought out or in the best interest of all children.

From Low Performing To Exemplary

The community gave me one of the highest ratings of any Durham Public Schools principal. When I walked into my first faculty conference for the 1999-2000 school year, I received a standing ovation. The National Alliance of Black School Educators gave me their prestigious Hall of Fame Ida B. Wells Risk Taker Award. It was a special treat being honored and receiving the award the same night as Desmond Tutu and the late Walter Patton. Durham Public Schools selected me as its Principal of The Year 2000. The Board of Education, City Council and County Commissioners read citations in my honor. Everyone was ecstatic, but me. I had reasons to be nervous. My gut instinct and observations told me that Southern was slipping back into bad habits and many of my directives were being ignored.

Again, too many students were engaging in the following at risk behavior:

Hall walking
Lateness to class
Sleeping
Coming to school without supplies
Not engaged in class work
In class without notebooks

I found myself consistently writing the same administrative directives or making morning announcements to stay the course with Best Practices that have a history of success:

Enforce the discipline policies
Require notebooks
Stop issuing passes unnecessary hall passes
Do not allow sleeping in class
Require all students to participate
Require note taking
Assign and mark homework
Help clear the halls
Focus on the curriculum
Use benchmark exams and analyze the data
Keep the focus on teaching and learning
Teach the entire period

Again, success is not a mystery. Ron Edmonds is highly regarded as one of the leaders of the "Effective Schools" movement. His philosophy is common sense. "We can, whenever and wherever we choose, successfully teach all children whose schooling is of interest to us. We already know more than we need to do that. Whether or not we do it must finally depend on how we feel about the fact that we haven't so far."

The problem with state mandated accountability models is nobody bears the blame but the principal and superintendent. Schools need to move away from site-based management and move to site-based accountability. Site-based management in theory is a good idea, but too often it becomes a political game played by power brokers. A brave step forward would be publishing the test scores of all teachers and forcing parents back into the process. Parents must be accountable, active players and not just critics of schools. Parents are given a free pass while the school officials are taking a beating in the press. Elected officials, parents and the media have demoralized and beaten teachers into submission and there are few qualified replacements. Politicians do not have the courage to hold parents accountable for student achievement. Instead of playing the blame game, it is time for educators, parents and students to assume equal accountability for developing a world-class school system. Schools within systems should share Best Practices. When things work, we hide them. Unfortunately, we still have children and stepchildren competing for recognition instead of working together as a collaborative team for children's sake.

Despite major flaws and work to be completed, Southern High School was one of the most improved schools in the state of North Carolina for the 1998-99 school year. This was a testament to the Herculean efforts of the SHS teachers, parents, students, counselors, staff and administrators. Even with success, we found ourselves way behind the rest of the state. Yet I was not able to enjoy it. I am reminded of the lessons learned from a man heralded as one of the world's greatest window washers. One day after washing windows on the 150th floor, he made the fatal mistake of taking three steps backward to admire his award winning work. Except for confirming that it can be done, the success of one year cannot guarantee you will be successful the next year. Thus, I issued a directive for the 1999-2000 school year:

The Exemplary Status Mandate of Best Practices 100%
Follow the School Improvement Plan
Teach the North Carolina Updated Standard Course of Study
Use Well Developed Lesson Plans
Teach Curriculum Aligned With Standardized Tests
Follow Pacing Guides
Administer Uniform Benchmark Exams
 Move from Lecture to Interactive Teaching
Teach To Various Learning Styles
Test What You Teach
Teach What You Test

100% Mandate for Students (Best Practices)
Follow School Policies
Complete Assigned homework
Organized Hard Notebooks
Note Taking-Record Daily Learning Objectives
Bar Charts Study Guides That Match Curriculum

Complacency, denial, fear, guilt, and the institutionalization of the status quo are dangerous norms for a school culture. The tragedy of life doesn't lie in not reaching goals. The unacceptable tragedy is that most people have no goals to reach. In God, we trust, but everyone else must bring data. Basically, people just work. Successful schools strive when administrators, teachers, board members, staff, students, and parents share a clear vision of what can be, expect excellence from themselves and others, and commit themselves to a process of continuous renewal. From diamonds in the rough, we can create crown jewels. But first we must believe!

There is nothing the Wizard gave Dorothy that she did not already have. Student achievement is higher, suspensions and discipline referrals are lower when expectations are high and discipline procedures are clearly defined, fair and consistent for all students. We must start the slow healing process of having faith in each other and ourselves. "Faith is the substance of things hoped for, the evidence of things not seen."

Southern Goes On The National Stage

Aleyah was healthy and expecting our third child! A boy! The press was granting me a honeymoon! During speaking engagements I was receiving standing ovations. My public opinion rating was sky high! Principal of the Year! Hall of Fame award! There is no way it could get better! What about a call from the White House? No, not the Big House, the White House!!!!

Mrs. Ramsey, my secretary called me over the walkie-talkie and stated I should call the superintendent immediately. Panic-stricken, I immediately returned the call. She informed me that representatives from the United States Education Department would be in the building in eight minutes. She further explained North Carolina Governor James Hunt was considering a Durham school as the site for the United States Education Secretary Richard Riley's Seventh Annual State of American Education Address!

A few weeks before Christmas of 1999, I received confirmation that Secretary Riley had chosen Southern. Quickly, I made an announcement over the school's public address system. I called

Aleyah and other family members. This was beyond my wildest dreams. No one gives a damn about the storm, but did you bring the ship in? The years of hard work, taking exams, lawsuits, threats on my life, sleeping in street clothes, unemployment, harsh and unrelenting criticism, and time away from my family was worth it! My God, I had promised the kids at Southern High School that we were going to shake up Durham, North Carolina, the nation and perhaps the world! My prediction was coming true! Why I had this unexplainable vision, I will never know, but I deeply believed the day would come when Southern High School would get on the national map.

North Carolina Governor James Hunt has earned a national reputation as the country's education governor. His leadership has led to extraordinary improvement in schools across the state. Teacher recruitment and retention, rigorous academic standards for students, Smart Start, early childhood academic intervention and raising the pay for North Carolina's professional educators came about because of Hunt's leadership. My assistant principal, John Benson asked for permission to coordinate the Riley visit. Benson was a 20-year army veteran and highly decorated Major. My job was to run the school. Benson's job was to make sure that 3,500 people and the national press came to Southern on February 22, 2000 and left singing our praises.

We met with local and national officials. Benson scheduled meetings and we reviewed agenda items. Every thing was carefully planned and we were consistently trouble-shooting. The response of the students, staff and community exceeded my loftiest vision of school community pride and dedication. We handled every adversity with speed and admirable acumen.

A week before the due date, I received notice that my Uncle William B. had died. I attended his funeral two days before our C-SPAN debut on national television. The wrinkles on my parents' faces showed the impact resulting from years of hard work, weariness, and raising five children. Despite being over seventy years of age, they are proud African Americans. My daddy cried like an innocent child at his brother's funeral. My mother comforted him and I provided a shoulder for my Uncle Johnny to lean on. My father's love and closeness to his dead brother brought the reality of my own mortality home to me. For the first time in my life, I became aware of his weakness, old age and vulnerability. At that moment, I forgave him for all the bad feelings I had held in my heart for much of my life. My daddy is human. Forgiveness is selfish. I did not forgive him for his sake. The cross was far too heavy for me to bear any longer. Most importantly, I looked at my father and realized that I had become him. I walked like him and I talked like him. He became my hero. When I consider it all, I realize I was wrong about him. You can't rewrite history. It is not good to throw stones when you live in a glass house, yourself.

Overall, he is the best man I have ever known. He raised 5 kids with a third grade education. Today, he works 6 days a week. He gets up at 5 in the morning and stops when it is dark. Hopefully, I will have his strength when I am his age. I love you, daddy. I have inherited his looks, mannerisms and facial expressions. In addition, the photographs in the living room clearly demonstrated that I was his twin. Thank you ma and pa for teaching me to walk with kings, but keep the common touch. I am glad I returned home and had an opportunity to spend some time with you as an adult. Now, I know why I returned to the South. I was able to bring closure to many childhood issues that I did not want to pass on to my children. We become what we think about most of the time. Thanks, God.

United States Education Department officials informed me that I had been allotted 4-5 minutes of speaking time during Education Secretary Riley's national address. For all of Pankey Town, I knew what I had to do. Peace and serenity replaced insecurity, fear and doubt. Aleyah was due to have the baby any day now. There was an ongoing bet that she would have the baby during Riley's speech.

At Southern, my secretary was getting hit with last minute emergencies and unexpected requests for tickets to Secretary Riley's speech. The staff and I agreed to have a normal uninterrupted school day. At a faculty conference, with a straight face, I asked the faculty and staff to conduct a normal school day. "I was willing to go into hell wearing a gasoline jacket to make the day a success!"

The day of the speech, I went to work at 5:30 a.m. I practiced every possible scenario. I concluded that I had received the world's best training at the N. C. School Of The Arts and felt ready. Several cars full of supporters from Laurinburg and Pankey Town came to see me before the speech. My parents, sisters and in-laws were in full force. My daddy purchased a new suit for the event and told everyone who would listen that he had a new $120.00 Stetson hat and he was the only "Negro" in Scotland County to have one. Prior to walking on the stage, I saw pride in my daddy's eyes and felt the warmth of unconditional love from my family. My seven-year-old daughter, Amira, whispered, "Make me proud."

The applause throughout my speech relaxed me and gave me momentary peace that I had not enjoyed for years. Our Superintendent, Dr. Ann Denlinger, whose success as an education leader had earned her the title of N.C. Superintendent of the Year, smiled. The school chorus and student body president delivered exemplary performances. North Carolina Governor James Hunt made an outstanding speech and praised my efforts as principal of Southern High School. The Governor told the audience that I had moved the school from Low Performing to Exemplary Status in one year. The United Education Secretary Richard Riley described me as a "principal on a mission." Riley's speech was delivered with energy, enthusiasm and indicative of wisdom and insights of a child-centered, sensitive, dedicated and wise education leader and statesman. February 22, 2000 was, perhaps, Henry Pankey, Pankey Town, Southern High School, Durham and the State of North Carolina's finest moment in time.

"From the cotton fields of North Carolina, I had finally made it to the national stage."

All press reports praised the fine-tuned meticulous organization and execution of the event. In essence, this description summarized popular opinion, "The seemingly flawless program was executed with military precision." Family members, guests and I retreated to my house after the event. My parents, sisters, in-laws, cousins, friends and I laughed about the national address. I felt proud for my parents. I was drained, but I felt great. From diamonds in the rough, we had become crown jewels! Yes!

The improvement of test scores at Southern High School represents one of the highlights of my career. A principal is only as good as the administrative team, teachers, counselors, staff, parents and students. The stakeholders came together at a significant moment in time and provided credibility to the belief system of statesman William Jennings Bryan when he said, "Destiny is not a matter of chance, it is a matter of choice; it is a thing to be waited for, it is a thing to be achieved." However, assistant principals John Benson, Beverley Wilson, William Graham, Dwight Womble and Dr. Joseph Settle's competence, dedication and loyalty greatly enhanced the possibility that our dream of an exemplary year was achieved.

March 11, 2000 Aleyah gave birth to our son, Aaron Kahlil Pankey. His innocent eyes were a joy to behold. Again, I found myself Standing in the Shadows of Greatness. Nothing during my lifetime prepared me for the feelings associated with the birth of my children.

She Devils

The story of two small girls often called She Devils is something that I often repeat during my speaking engagements:

There were these two little girls who decided to play a trick on their 80-year-old Granddaddy. They knew that he could barely see, had difficulty hearing and was weak and feeble. They decided to put a baby bird in each hand and ask him which hand the baby bird was in. As soon as he picked a hand, they planned to squeeze the bird until it was dead. They said, "Granddaddy, which hand do we have the baby bird in?" Granddaddy ignored the little girls, because they were mean little girls. So mean, he often called them she-devils. They continued. "Granddaddy, please play with us and tell us which hand we have the baby bird in. Granddaddy, please." Granddaddy looked for his spit cup.....cause he had to spit....ya know when you dip snuff...the kind with the railroad on the can, you know what I mean...it sometimes run down the side of your face and you need your cup...cause it gets nasty and you have to spit and you need that little red hankerchief too,...gets kind of nasty....They continued. "Granddaddy, which hand do we have the bird in?" Granddaddy continued to ignore the girls and flipped his toupee off...'cause his head was getting hot and sweat was running down the side of his face. They kept yelling and pulling on Granddaddy and asking "which hand do we have the baby bird in" but he continued to ignore the little girls and used his toothpick to stir up the snuff cause it loses its flavor and the toothpick makes it taste more better. The girls started dancing around granddaddy, pulling him and asking "which hand do we have the baby bird in?" Granddaddy grabbed both girls and held them close. They were mean little girls and continued with their game and chants: "Granddaddy, Granddaddy which hand do we have the baby bird in?" Granddaddy looked at the little girls with tears in his eyes and said, "The baby bird's life is in your hands!"

That's where we are. The lives of children are in the hands of adults. All decisions must be made based on what is in the best interest of children.

We Must Fight For Our Children

Many reforms that focus on increasing the achievement of minority students are hopelessly misguided by a lack of courage. They mean well, but lack the courage to take on education malpractice issues. Superintendents under contract last approximately two years before they are fired. Teachers are afraid of principals. Principals are afraid of superintendents. Superintendents are afraid of parents. School board members are afraid of voters. Undisciplined kids are afraid of no one. Consequently, the best intended school reform effort very quickly hit a glass ceiling. We should not be afraid to discipline disruptive pupils that raise holy hell in school. They, too, are hurting and looking for us to save them. Children cannot run schools. We also need to take off the gloves and jack up the derogatory rap artists, jailhouse-influenced culture, magazines, and celebrities that teach sleaze. We should also confront radio and television shows that are corrupting the minds of our youth. Why are we afraid of them? They are not afraid of us and are making billions of dollars exploiting our children. We will spend millions of dollars on school restructuring and "all children can learn" and "high expectations" slogans, but lack the moral courage to mandate that all students bring notebooks,

books, paper and pencils to school. Jerry Springer teaches our kids sex education and the 300 billion dollar rap industry tells them what to wear. Gang members control the colors and do rags and dress code for many school children. Don't deny the existence of gangs. It is a tragic mistake to ignore the warning signs. Principals have a right to mandate a dress code. We consistently play Russian roulette with the lives of children until a Columbine type mass killing temporarily wakes us up. School tragedies usually cause a knee-jerk reaction that lasts about a month. We react to the murder of our babies as if it is a movie. Let's stand. Let's fight. Children cannot fight for themselves.

The behavior of teachers at Southern was professional, committed and dedicated to school improvement. However, complacency was slowly creeping back into the school's culture. Excellent teachers were busting their butts. Some of our best teachers retired. New teachers were not prepared for the challenge of at risk students. Far too many students went to class without notebook, paper, and pencils. The core teaching strategy involved lecture, despite repeated pleas to move from lecture to interactive teaching and learning.

Effective teacher training is the only solution. Teachers are trained by lecture-oriented professors. The universities are not doing an adequate job preparing our new teachers. College professors haven't been inside a public school since their graduation from high school. We have a colossal mismatch. Why not hire school administrators and classroom teachers as adjunct professors?

The teaching delivery model of the teachers at Southern High School is the norm for high school teachers around the country. Lecture is used as a form of transmitting information and a means of control. Discipline is a problem in many high schools. Teachers have a right to teach and students have a right to learn. Teachers are shy about assuming the role of disciplinarian. Teachers are overworked, underpaid and under-appreciated. They don't need political posturing. They don't need new standardized tests. They need the support of administrators, staff development, parental support, better pay and parents dedicated to sending well-disciplined students to school on time each day.

The overwhelming majorities of kids are wonderful and try very hard to do the right thing every day. We owe it to them to maintain a wholesome and safe environment that is conducive to teaching and learning. Discipline procedures, security precautions and rules may appear to be punitive. However, gangs hurt the progress of student achievement. Most new gang members come from our middle schools. The recruiters are in high school or older men out of school. Of the high schools in Durham, Southern, probably had the lowest gang memberships. They hindered Southern and are negatively impacting school improvement across the country. Their containment was far too time-consuming. They were dealt with very quietly and without fanfare, but they are a cancer that has caused a sore full of acid that is rotten to the bone.

Gangs - At Risk Student Behavior

Gangs are in our public schools. Although, most officials and parents would like to ignore their existence, they are a serious threat to school safety as well as student achievement. They will not volunteer to go away. In addition, they are very time-consuming and create gridlock that forces administrators to focus on them instead of academic improvement. They wear their colors and bandanas. They don't bluff. They will kill you. They use threats and intimidation to control classrooms, halls, bathrooms, school buses, cafeterias, playgrounds and neighborhoods. All students who dress the same are not in gangs. However, students dressing the same is not always a fad or accident. When do we learn? You must know your kids!

Gang membership for young men requires stealing, selling drugs or guns, beating innocent victims or killings as ordered by generals. Girls engage in the same activities, but sex is at the top of the list. One female student confessed to having oral sex with 25 members of a gang. This was part of her initiation orientation. Her situation was like the roach motel. She was in, but could not get out. Let's keep it real. Girls in gangs have sex with gang members. Boys sell drugs, beat up, shoot, stab or kill people.

Kids in gangs and those not affiliated with gangs dress the same way. The difference is hard-core criminal activity and discipline problems. However, every child engaged in inappropriate behavior is not in a gang. Boy, do we have a mess!

Parents are too often in deep denial and will verbally attack a school official if such accusations against their children are brought to their attention. Principals are afraid to tell school officials, because they may get the blame for having gang members in their schools. I was often accused of hyperbole or sensationalism. I was also accused of having a suspension or expulsion hit list. However, I knew my gang members and met with them as gang members. Henry Pankey does not play with gang members. They were not allowed to control the safe and orderly school environment that we created in our school. All children deserve a safe school. Principals, parents, school officials unaware of who's in gangs are headed for serious trouble. You will definitely have a series of fights, riots and brazen bullies intimidating other students. If the other students do not believe in your ability to protect them, they will do what they have to do to protect themselves. Good kids will bring weapons to school. Middle class parents and school officials don't understand because they think middle class. This is street stuff. Safety is the one thing that is non-negotiable. Despite letters, notes in notebooks, police reports, graffiti on desks, bathroom walls or vacant buildings, most community members believe that gangs are something that bad kids somewhere else engage in. Not my child. If it hits home, the rationale is that their child hangs out with the wrong crowd and/or is in the wrong place at the wrong time. Water seeks its own level. Birds of a feather do flock together.

One thing for sure, sexually transmitted diseases are not spread by reading books. Videos do not cause teen pregnancy. The escalation of violence and teen pregnancies are sometimes, but not always, connected to gangs. Trips to the hospital, morgue and cemetery are real. Keep your eyes on the newspapers. Read the obituaries. Pay careful attention to big fights in schools, rap concerts or athletic events. Notice the drive by and random killings of young people. They are not random. There is no such thing as being at the wrong place at the wrong time. Gang bangers know their targets. Sex causes pregnancy. There is no such thing as an accidental pregnancy. Teenagers like to look like each other and emulate images from the media. We have a very serious problem trying to figure out who is in a gang and who is wearing the latest teen fashion. Again, students that are not in gangs dress like those that are members. Virgins dress like girls that are promiscuous. Rap artists and gangs influence fashions. All rap artists are not bad. They are not thugs, but they should not be the role models for our children. Our famous money hungry designers are stealing styles from the jails, projects and streets. They don't give a damn about our children. Money rules! How smart do you have to be to design clothes that make you look half naked, expose your underwear and fall off when you walk? Hootchie is as hootchie does!

As a principal, I believe in dealing with facts and making judgments based on very intensive investigations. Experience has taught me that students rarely lie to the principal one on one. Despite my reputation as a strict hard nosed-disciplinarian, students are my most reliable sources for accurate information. This has been a consistent pattern for over 25 years. We cannot continue to ignore the problems of our children. We can no longer pretend things are going to return to the good ole days. The blame game must cease. Professional educators and parents need to work together and learn the "socialization" culture of teenagers in the 21st century.

Below Expectations

During my tenure at Southern we achieved Exemplary Status, met State Expected Gains, but, despite improvements, we missed the state's goals by one tenth of a point for the 2000-2001 school year. We missed the state standards by about one tenth of a point. How much of the loss was gang related? What about excessive tardies? Absences? Lack of notebooks? No paper? No pencils or pens? What's the negative impact of students registering for school six months after the start date?

Nothing counts but the outcome! The state of North Carolina gave us "Safe School" recognitions three years in a row. We also reduced fights, increased student achievement, enhanced school morale, cut the dropout rate, raised scholarship money, and dramatically increased the number of students attending college. The media gave us accolades for innovative and successful improvements. It harshly reprimanded us when we did not achieve state expectations. None of us is perfect. I am forever grateful for the support, dedication and flexibility of the Southern High School community, students and staff. We are family. Durham County's ever shifting politics was about to bring my tenure at Southern High School to a dramatic end.

Throughout my days at Southern, I consistently heard rumors that I would become the principal of Hillside High School in Durham, North Carolina. Hillside is known as one of the state's only remaining traditional Black High Schools. It is sparsely integrated; it is still commonly referred to as a Black School. Hillside has a national reputation as a school that has produced many accomplished African Americans. Most notable among them was the NBA and tennis star John Lucas. Its alumni ranks include senators, doctors, lawyers, dentists, teachers, prominent and successful businessmen and CEO's. Tradition and pride aptly personify Hillside. Like many urban schools, Hillside faces the challenge of improving the academic achievement of its students.

Transferred To Hillside High School

In August 2000, a parent accused Hillside's principal of changing grades to insure her son's eligibility to play football. Durham public schools conducted an intensive investigation that inflamed the Hillside community. The racial split was intense, hostile and divisive. Eventually a decision was made to hire a principal from Chatham County, but that arrangement fell apart as he decided that he did not want the job. Rumors continued that I would become the new principal. Members of the Southern community wanted me to stay at Southern and

123

Hillside supporters wanted to keep their principal at the helm. June 1, 2001, I reported to work on my first day as principal of Hillside High School.

The rumors began to flood throughout the community that I was bringing over 20 teachers with me. They also indicated that I had the police take a teacher out of the building in handcuffs. Rumors are a potent weapon, because you cannot fight a ghost. Every denial or attempt to achieve vindication magnifies the rumor. The summer transition was very difficult because of the loss of two veteran administrators and the hiring of novices in my administration. Rumors and scheduling problems plagued me throughout the summer and did not abate before the opening of school. Emotions boiled over. The media coverage was extensive.

Remember, there is a price you pay for being well known. The gods do not give you fame for free. I was well trained by the media of New York City. Although I did not like the attacks on my administration, the media quoted the pro and con sentiments of the community. The low performing designation of Southern High School, inaccurate and incomplete schedules, fear, rumors and unrelenting support for the previous principal presented seemingly insurmountable obstacles. However, there was never a time when I did not believe that the school and community were ready to move forward. How do we put the pain, fear, suspicions, gossip and doubt behind us? We must heal. "It is because it resists change that we say pride goeth before the fall." The feedback and messages I received were consistently ambivalent. The rumors were very precise:

Pankey was going to bring more than 20 teachers
    over from Southern
A teacher was taken out of the building in handcuffs
He hired his girlfriend as one of his assistant principals
He is a dictator
He does not listen
He blows the whistle in the ears of students
A secretary is doing teacher evaluations
He talks at least 10 minutes a day on the P.A. system
He searched a female student's purse, removed a sanitary
    napkin, held it up, laughed and asked students if it
    looked like a weapon

He is anti-intellectual
He is an Uncle Tom
He is a plantation Negro
He is a flunky for the Superintendent
He treats and evaluates whites better than Blacks
He is loud
He is going to bring the school down
He will increase the suspension rate
He disrespects students, parents, teachers and the staff

You name the rumor and resistance to change and you can place it beside my name. You may even be lucky enough to get it in the newspapers. The rumors and debates become a part of a toxic culture that stymies change, school reform and success.

Of course, everybody claims that they want a change, but it cannot be accomplished by doing the same things the same way with a different outcome. Einstein once stated, "Insanity is doing the same thing but expecting different results." We know that if we keep doing the same thing, we will get the same results, but we keep doing the same things and blame the outcome on change agents such as reformers.

Hello! Despite all the politics and passion that we use to lay on our swords, there are at risk children who need us to work together. Children will not improve test scores until they bring notebooks and books to school. Schools must have rules. Children have the right to a safe and orderly environment conducive to teaching and learning. Parents must help. Educators and parents must work together. All decisions must be made based on what is in the best interest of children. We either believe all children can learn or we don't. We either love all children unconditionally or we don't. It is just that simple.

School is not going back to the way it was when adults were children. Standardized tests are here to stay. Technology rules for real. The future is unstoppable. It's not about Black and white anymore. It's not about immigrants. It's not about special education children. It's not about adults. It is about a marketable education learned in a safe and wholesome environment for all children. It's called tough love and the focus is on love. It's called unconditional love. We do the best we can, because children are reason enough.

We cannot continue to say we love children and not require them to bring notebooks, books, paper and pencils to school. Bringing books to school will not sentence children to back pains for life. We must mandate effective classroom instruction. Student achievement is a must. Failure is not an option.

Principles are more important than being principal. Perhaps I will always be controversial, but I still believe in the following Best Practices:

Safe and orderly school
Effective teaching
Follow the standard course of study

Benchmark exams
Well-developed lesson plans
Curriculum aligned with standardized tests
Strong leadership
Research-based best practices with a history of success
Enforce student-centered discipline
Hard notebooks full of paper
Good manners
High visibility
Frequent monitoring of classroom instruction
Test what you teach
Teach what you test
Pens and pencils

Character education
Walking to the right
Pledge of allegiance
Silence or some form of meditation/reflection each day
Books for all children
Qualified teachers/administrators
Children cannot run a school
Zero tolerance for violence
Benevolent disciplinarians
Addressing learning styles
Laptop computers for all High School students
Teaching the curriculum
Flexible lessons

Infusion of technology across the curriculum
Reading across the curriculum
Homework each night
Aligning the curriculum with standardized tests
Ongoing data analysis
Best practices
Cultural diversity
Multidimensional exams based on Multiple Intelligences
Standardized tests
Literacy centers in all schools
Equity of outcomes
Unconditional love for all children

Adults are in charge of the school
Faith that all children can learn
Metal detectors
Security cameras
College money for all high school graduates
Dress for success
A reasonable dress code

Parental involvement
High expectations
Kids don't tell grown folks what to do

We will have cycles of success and failure. Success and failure are inevitable parts of school reform and school improvement. National data indicates that schools and   institutional reforms have a history of ups and downs. It is a fact of life. All champions win and lose. Champs get off the mat and fight until the end even if it is toe to toe. Great men respond to defeat and use it as inspiration to get better, because good leaders know that failure should be a motivator instead of an undertaker. Dr. King once stated, "Only when it is dark enough can you see the stars." Education is about teaching children how to overcome failure. School or real world politics will never go away. Dr. King also said, "True peace is not the absence of tension, but the presence of justice."

Near the end of the 2002 school year the Hillside staff came together and began giving me support that I had hoped to receive in August 2001. My ultimate concern was pondering if it was too little, too late. Maybe, test scores would ultimately deicide my future and the state's ranking of the school. The central office was closely monitoring the day-to-day operations. Many staff members were visibly upset. Although, we had come together as a family, we had a lot of work to complete. A series of letters, rumors and personnel meetings began to take its toll on my administration and the Hillside staff. The community had concluded that I was being undermined by the central office and my days were numbered.

My mother's health deteriorated dramatically. I found out that both my parents had cancer. My father had prostate cancer and my mother discovered cancer in both breasts. My decision to move back to the South was a good one. It was important to get to know my parents, be helpful and learn to understand and appreciate the good and bad of my childhood. Now, I can forgive and be a supportive son. Perhaps, all children regret not paying more attention to their parents and not showing gratitude for their sacrifices.

My mother's face was etched with all the sorrow, pain, fatigue and weariness of the years of hard work and worry. Slowly, she is quietly and peacefully going into that good night of peace and serenity. Yes, parting is such sweet and bitter sorrow. Over the years I have read hundreds of books or articles about positive thinking and exemplary role models. Never have I seen or heard of a person with the unflinching and unconquerable courage of my mother. Undoubtedly, cancer is painful. She refused to complain. Instead of perceiving herself as a victim, she talked about being thankful for all that God has given her and the time she has been allowed to spend on this earth. This remarkable woman worked over 35 years cleaning bedpans as a nurse's aide. She rejoiced at the opportunity to serve and help the sick. During every visit to her at home or in the hospital I deliberately looked for a crack in her armor. It never happened. She truly believes that Jesus Christ is the son of God and she will die and go to heaven. She believes that God is in charge and His Will shall be done. There is no turning back.

My father fought a courageous fight with prostate cancer. He too, never complained. It is not about me. It is about family. Who are Mamie and Jesse Pankey? I have looked all over the world for heroes and role models and they were in the heart of Pankey Town all along. David Pankey is the respected mayor of Pankey Town. My sisters Pat, Jessie and Betty have the faith of saints. My stepbrother Frank has returned home to take care of my Aunt Carrie Lee. He and my cousins Myra Green II and James W. McNeill are doing a wonderful job as caretakers of my mother, father, and aunts. My brother James is a master carpenter. My Uncle Henry, Uncle Johnny, Aunt Carrie Lee, Aunt Edith, Aunt Nettie, and Aunt Myra have emerged as bigger heroes than any others in history books. Beulah Monley is the unsung hero who took me to school my first year at Scotland High School. The white bus drove by me everyday. My cousin Jerome has become a millionaire. He currently resides in Maryland. Without his support, I never would have graduated from the University of Maryland. My cousin David Pankey, Jr. was an important source of faith, strength and inspiration during my days at the North Carolina School of The Arts. I was blessed that David was in WinstonSalem during my undergraduate years. David is an extraordinary jazz pianist. My wife, Aleyah has taught my children Aaron, Amira and Ashia the importance of unconditional love. These people are all remarkable. The Pankeys come from good stock.

We become our parents. Self-pity, wallowing in misery, and abandoning faith is not part of my make up. Mamie Pankey's unconditional love, courage, tenacity and faith made me what I am. Even I cannot change my history and history determines the outcome. Every thought, every touch, every statement, and every experience makes us who we are. Adversity is basic training for courage, determination and persistence. Mamie Pankey is an imperfect mother sent on a perfect mission. However, she was the right mother for her children. Four out of six of her kids went to college. That speaks for itself.

Many Blacks have become middle class and want history to ignore our past:
   Unconquerable seeds of greatness
   Bootleggers/dope dealers
   Slavery
   Hard work
   Beauty
   Weekend drunkenness of relatives

Church on Sundays
Spending a week's paycheck in 24 hours
Smelling like day old liquor
The hootchie cootchie women
Marriages at an early age
Children born out of wedlock
Racism
Poverty
Strong families with a good mama and daddy
Love of God
Patriotism
Debt
Welfare
Outdoor toilets
Farm work
Pride
Dignity
Geniuses
Self Respect
Love
Hard work
Historical giants
Extraordinary athletic ability
Fervent & unshakeable faith in God
God sits high and looks low
First ones to finish high school
First one to finish college
First one to build a brick house
Extraordinary intelligence

Remember the whole history and we will realize that we are no better and/or worse than anybody else in the world. We have a rich and noble history. We should be proud of our history. Yes, we have a long ways to go, but we have come a great distance. We have nothing to be ashamed of. In essence, good, bad or indifferent, people are all basically the same.

As the year at Hillside came to an end, rumors intensified that I would be replaced. Coincidentally, I received a call from a New York City Superintendent. He indicated that the Chancellor of New York City public schools was interested in someone developing a discipline plan for 1,200 schools. My name was on a short list. Consequently, I went to New York City and met with Chancellor Harold Levy On June 10, 2004 regarding a high profile position as Deputy Superintendent of Discipline. He indicated that he was seriously considering me for the position. This represented an extraordinary career move for me. The job would entail the supervision of discipline procedures for 1.2 million students. However, the specificity of the job and description was still in the planning stage. A New York Superintendent informed me the Chancellor wanted to hire me. Returning to New York would have added thousands of dollars to my retirement pension.

The same week, the New York State legislature gave New York's Mayor Michael Bloomberg greater control of the school system. He was given authorization to create a reformatted Board Of Education. A few days later, published reports indicated that Harold Levy was replaced by new Chancellor Joel Klein. Chancellor Klein would bring his own staff. Throughout this process, I kept my Superintendent abreast of all the given circumstances. Published reports indicated a new principal and administrative team would assume the leadership at the school. The principal and assistant principals would be given new assignments. Many teachers, counselors, support staff, secretaries and janitors would also receive a transfer to another site. Hillside students met the state expectations and requirements on the state mandated end of the year tests. In addition, the school has never been rated as low performing. At the time, the scores were the highest in the school's history.

Parents, staff, residents, students, the Committee on the Affairs of Black People, the NAACP, the Hillside PTSA, the Site Based Committee and religious organizations passionately protested the personnel changes. Charges of racism, nepotism and conspiracy theories dominated conversations and news reports for a long period of time. If all of us think alike, then somebody's not thinking.

The Black community has looked back at the history of school integration and wondered if it was a good idea. Many Black schools have lost their history as a result of integration. Hillside's history includes movers and shakers that have made extraordinary contributions to society:

College professors
Judges
Politicians
Legendary track Coach Russell Blunt
Record setting track stars
Educator John Lucas, Sr.
Professional athletes
Senators
Architects
Millionaires
Doctors
Lawyers
Designers
Artists
Nationally acclaimed theatre program
World-class marching band
Exemplary educators
Exemplary status/recognition on standardized tests

Blacks believe that the best way to preserve a historical legacy is to maintain control. Slavery, racism, poor student achievement, dropouts, push outs, suspensions, expulsions have angered Blacks all over the country. Although, many are not as vocal as the Hillside community, they feel the same way. The tinkering with Black history, culture, community values, and the soul of the human spirit, and belief system that all Black children can excel has raised suspicion in the African-American neighborhoods. It is not about the exclusivity of test scores. It is about the salvation of our children. It is about the realization that our children live to be 70 years old. What will they know and be able to do? What type of citizens will they become? Will they have marketable skills? Will they get jobs? Will Black girls be able to find a husband? Will they see the beauty in themselves? Will they know their history? Will they develop spiritually? Again, the words of Dr. Martin Luther King, Jr. seem to summarize the given circumstances. "True peace is not the absence of tension, but the presence of justice." When people perceive there is no justice, they will insure that there is no peace. No justice-no peace. Know justice-know peace. The words of Robert G. Ingersoll are wise and pragmatic. "Justice is the only worship. Love is the only priest. Ignorance is the only slavery. Henry W. Longfellow provides additional enlightenment. "If we could read the secret history of our enemies, we should find in each man's life sorrow and suffering enough to disarm all hostility."

Making me out to be some kind of stupid, Uncle Tom boogey man cannot have a positive impact on the children at Hillside. Planting an onslaught of letters in the newspapers will not impact student achievement. Dedication to school improvement and research-based education innovations, with a history of success, will move student achievement to a higher level.

Equipped with the ever changing fashions, super rich media stars, nervously checking report cards and transcripts, our children are still on the sidelines at tiptoe stance weeping with their faces pressed hard against glass ceilings Standing in the Shadows of Greatness!

Rising From The Ashes

Another school district offered me a pay raise and a job as principal in Long Island, New York. I declined the offer. I was reassigned to Carrington Middle School as an assistant principal. This time, I embraced the words of Richard Henley:

It matters not how strait the gate
How charged with punishment the scroll
I am the master of my fate
I am the captain of my soul

The year's experience at Carrington turned out to be a Godsend. My family bonded closer together. A leader is only as good as the people that surround him/her. The staff was incredible. Lorraine Tuck and Chris Bennet are excellent administrators. James Key, the principal, was extremely supportive. He has earned my lifelong respect. Mr. Key ranks high as one of the best educators I have been associated with during my career. He assigned me to the 6th grade. The teachers and I fell in love with each other. My giddy sense of humor returned. I supervised the 6th grade. The 6th grade as well as the rest of the school received the best test scores in the school's history.

The year was one of the most relaxed years I've had in the last 25 years. Guidance counselor Frank O'Neal became a very important friend, confidant and therapist. He kept my focus on using my skills to support the staff and children. Carrington is an exemplary school that has institutionalized the attributes of an effective student-centered place of learning. The North Carolina Department of Public Instruction recognized Carrington as a School Of Distinction for the 2002-2003 school year. The quintessential educators deserve the honor. Carrington reenergized me and restored my faith in education.

Test scores continue to improve at Scotland, Southern, and Hillside High Schools, but Dr. Susan S. McKinney JHS 265 in New York is still plagued with violence and chronic low test scores. Dress for Success, dress code restrictions, metal detectors, video cameras, zero tolerance, and uniform enforcement of strict discipline codes are gaining widespread acceptance by the public, and school officials. Student achievement is higher in a student centered safe and orderly environment conducive to teaching and learning.

As Shakespeare's King Lear once said, "Ingratitude is the greatest of all sins." I would be remiss if I did not thank the extraordinary, competent, and loyal educators who have stood by me as destiny, providence and coincidence have tossed this embattled vessel into the many treacherous waters of life's restless seas. Highly competent educators at Hillside such as Dan Gilfort, Chris Brewington, Rashad Ali, Carolyn Wallace, Robert Massey, LaVerne Mattocks, department leaders, teachers and staff members kept our focus on making decisions that were in the best interest of children.

Patrick Rhodes, Barbara Simmons, Bill Graham, Chalice Yehling, Jamie Ramsey, Don Ramsey, Pete Shankle, Jessica Harris, Cheryl Bogues-Munn, and Ann Ringer are student centered educators and very supportive friends. Friends like Bob and Buena Wheless have taught my family the importance of unshakeable faith. I am deeply indebted to Durham Public Schools, the community, educators, students and parents for giving me an opportunity to share my expertise and vision. Durham's test scores are consistently improving.

My life ministry is to help low performing children. The words of Napoleon Hill still resonate in my mind:

> *A careful inventory of all your past experiences may disclose the startling fact that everything has happened for the best....I am thankful for the adversities which have crossed my pathway, for they have taught me tolerance, sympathy, self-control, perseverance, and some other virtues I might never have known.*

The North Carolina Department of Public Instruction-School Improvement Division has hired me as a member of the State Assistance Team. The State Assistance Team members are assigned to Low Performing schools in need of improvement. The team's mission is help increase student achievement, and build capacity in a manner that will institutionalize permanent success strategies. This is a position that I have coveted for years. North Carolina has earned a national reputation as a result of effective innovations in the area of school improvement. This successful model is studied by educators across the county. This is an excellent opportunity to work with some of the country's top experts in the academic arena.

I share the determination and faith of Helen Keller:
I am only one;
But still I am one.
I cannot do everything,
But still I can do
Something; I will not
Refuse to do the
Something I can do.

Timing is an essential component of good leadership. Leaders need to be flexible. They also need to know when to move on.

Good Friday Always Comes Before Easter

Principles are more important than being principal. My Mama taught me that evil may get the headlines, but God still sits on the throne.

Mamie McDuffie Pankey, Jesse Pankey, Harriet Tubman, Malcolm X, Sojourner Truth, Martin Luther King, Jr., Mary McLeod Bethune, the great educator Benjamin Mays, James Comer, Pankey Town and my ancestors are my heroes. My heroes are not on television or in the news. My Aunt Edith Pankey has provided me words of wisdom and encouragement throughout my life. Aunt Edith is an unsung hero, motivator and role model. My sister Patricia Pankey Owens is my role model as an educator. Nobody personifies the spirit of forgiveness and a love of humanity better than my wife Aleyah.

About a century years ago, My Grandfathers Luther Frank McDuffie and Tom Pankey went into partnership with Tom's brothers Sam and Dan Pankey. They purchased 100 acres of land referred to as a "cullud folks community" that included sixteen families. Pankey Town was born. Grandfather, Luther Frank McDuffie made the bricks used to build his house. He solved math problems and did the measurements in his head without paper or pencil. Family members currently live in the house. When I think of the origins of Pankey Town my mind races back to the cotton fields of 1960. My fellow cotton pickers are hot, tired, sweating and although their clothes are sticking to their gleaming bodies, they continue to pick from can see to can't see. Blisters on their hands and swollen ankles are ignored. The sun beats down like a jealous and angry goddess from the intestinal walls of hell. The snakes are a menace. Mosquitoes and yellow flies are biting and collecting blood as if they work for the Red Cross. Liquid pain runs down the side of their faces. Ice water is a precious commodity. At lunchtime pork and beans are a delicacy. Folks would fight over a Pepsi and honey bun. Nobody complained. Who would have thought that Pankey

Town's last set of cotton pickers would make their mark in the world:

Charles McDuffie, Doctor of Law Degree
Pauline McDuffie, Teacher
Patricia Pankey, MBA, Teacher
Mamie McDuffie, Beautician
Betty Pankey, Daycare Teacher
Jessie Lee Pankey, Minister
Annie Margaret Monley, Teacher
Eddie Pankey, Master Brick Mason
James A. Pankey, Master Carpenter
Eddie Frank Pankey, Owner of Cleaning Services
Alvin Pankey, Vietnam War Hero
Anthony Jerome Pankey, Millionaire-Businessman
David Pankey, Jr., CEO BellSouth, Jazz Recording Artist
Ruth Jean Pankey, BFA Fayetteville State University
Elaine Green, Teacher
David Pankey, Mayor of Pankey Town

Miracles were growing in those cotton fields.

My soul is radiating with the essence of the Negro Spiritual, "Ain't Nothing Gonna Turn Me Around."

I still believe lessons learned at Allen Chapel Church in Pankey Town:

There is still a balm in Gilead to heal the wounded soul.

The arch of the moral universe is long, but it bends toward justice.

You reap what you sow.

You live by the sword and you die by the sword.

Weeping may endure for the night, but joy cometh in the morning.

Good Friday comes before Easter.

The cross comes before the crown.

The crucifixion comes before the resurrection.

There is a day of resurrection

Gabriel's trumpet has signaled onward charge and knows not a note of retreat.

Agony, ecstasy, pain, gain, fear, doubt, family, success, and failure have taught me to dream, but not make dreams my master. It is noble to walk with kings, but it's nobler to keep the common touch. Unconditional love means the love does not have to be returned. Shallow incidents are not important, but children are! It's not about me. It's about children. Fight for children. We can't sit this one out.

Be willing to lose your job for your principles. Advocates for children will always find a job! I am willing to lose all that I have for my beliefs and unconditional love for our children. Unapologetically, I am who I am. When my day comes, I just want to be able to stand before the God of this universe and say, "Master, I have tried to fight the good fight. I have finished my course. I have kept the faith. I am asking for your mercy and forgiveness. I am ready for your judgment."

Although the art of wordsmith may betray me, this anonymous poem summarizes my core beliefs:

I am tired of sailing my little boat
Far inside the harbor bar
I want to go out where the big ships float
Out on the deep where the great ones are
And should my frail craft prove too slight
For waves that sweet the pillars ore
I'll rather go down in a stirring fight
Than drown to death by the sheltered shore

The only credentials I have are myself. Finally, I find myself Standing in the Shadows of Greatness!

People Are Talking About Henry Pankey

"Pankey knows something about change. He has maintained order and structure even in the most chaotic of places." Lottie Joyner, American School Board Journal

"North Carolina Newspapers have lionized Pankey as a no nonsense benevolent disciplinarian capable of turning around out of control and low performing schools." The Carolina Times

"One of the great educators in New York History." Joseph Lentol, New York State Assemblyman

"Principal of Dr. Susan S. McKinney Junior High School 265 in Brooklyn, N. Y. since 1992, Pankey has transformed his school from the fifth most violent in the city to one of the safest in the state. He is credited with restoring dignity and calm and enhancing the educational process of this troubled school by using tough love." Winston Salem Chronicle

"I realized there was already something starting to happen that I hadn't seen before in my many visits to dozens of different schools. Pankey was adding a Fourth R to the traditional reading, riting and rithmetic. It was called Respect." Jon Naso, Photo Journalist, New York Newsday

This school under Principal Henry Pankey, has shown how much we can improve public schools with the right leadership... this school went from Low Performing one year to Exemplary Growth the next year...in one year, that's what you can do." James B. Hunt, Jr., Governor of North Carolina

"I have never seen anybody quite like him. His voice....his oratorical skills are unique. Once you get to know him, you realize that he has formidable substance." Obah Ward, Former

PTSA President, Boys And Girls High School, Brooklyn, New York; New York Amsterdam News

"Tough talking, no nonsense Henry Pankey...is every ill behaved, unmotivated student's nightmare. But Pankey is every parent's dream in this unsettled age of schoolhouse massacres, failing discipline and anemic academic achievement." Raleigh News And Observer

"Disciplined, diligent, reliable, tough, eloquent, generous, fearless, brilliant, talented, loving, caring. (The list could go on and in no particular order.)" Lesley Hunt, Master Speech Instructor, University Of N. C. School Of The Arts

"He always put God first. And he knew He would lead the way. He was blessed to be able to do the things he wanted to do." Mamie Pankey, Mother, Laurinburg Exchange

"We have better attendance in school. More kids come on time. More teachers are collaborating and working with students who need help." Jane Cheeseborough, Representative, United Federation Of Teachers, New York City

"Scotland High School students scored an average of 17 points higher on the 1997 Scholastic Aptitude Test (SAT) than they did the year before." Laurinburg Exchange

"The total score improvement for 1997 was the largest at Scotland High in the last five years." Dr. John Batchelor, Superintendent, Laurinburg Exchange

"Henry Pankey is a man of true character who welcomes a challenge and dedicates his talent toward achieving noble goals." Paula Mann, Parent, Durham, N. C.

"We needed a strong person here. He has a positive direction for our children. They were getting lost far between the cracks." Bertha Smith, Community Activist, Brooklyn, New York, New York Newsday

"Steve Littenberg, District Supervisor for school safety officers, said JHS 265 is now one of the safest schools in New York City." Laurinburg Exchange

"End of test scores, among worst in the Triangle last year, surged ahead in 10 of 11 categories after the first semester." Raleigh News And Observer

Pankey's transformation of Southern High School from a school with academic and discipline problems to a respected high school is well documented. Pankey is in many ways the modern version of the legendary principal-taskmasters of days past, who expected students to come to school scrubbed and ready to learn. Durham Herald Sun

"Brilliant." Robert Murray, Master Drama Instructor, University Of North Carolina School Of The Arts

"Thanks to Principal Pankey for doing a superb job at Southern. My family is behind him." Vinny Abbruseato, Parent, Durham, N. C.

"Mr. Pankey has a proven track record of successful leadership.... He has a participatory leadership style and he values teachers and often involves the community as a resource for his programs." Sonja Leathers, North Carolina Department Of Public Instruction, Bridging the Gap

"He's special, like a diamond in the sky." Dyan Barton, Assistant Principal, Tilden High School, Brooklyn, New York, New York Amsterdam News

"I've seen bad years when there was no such thing as order, other year things calmed down, but this is the first time I've seen consistency in the tone of the school." Helen Henderson, coordinator at JHS 265, 35 year veteran educator. New York Newsday

"Henry Pankey is one of the most dedicated and competent administrators that I have ever known. In the halls he is a boundless source of energy that inspires students to believe in themselves. His enthusiasm and his love for education permeates everything that transpires in his school." Luisa Haynes, Parent-Educator, North Carolina

"A man with a multi-faceted intellectual persona, Henry shows that the core of his educational philosophy is predicated on his belief in the dignity and worth of every human being. He frequently refers to students whose potential has not yet been tapped as diamonds in the rough. Henry is indeed a master jeweler who is capable of using his pearls of wisdom to perfect the gems in his care." Linda Douglas, School Administrator, North Carolina

"Mr. Pankey is a great motivator. He has an uncanny ability to get total support from students, faculty and staff, parents and the community members." Barry E. Wall, Ed.D, Principal, Lee County High School, Sanford, North Carolina

"The institution of the Dress For Success program has been a driving force to heighten student self esteem. Mr. Pankey awarded Medals of Achievement to each faculty and staff member for attaining Exemplary Status months prior to actual testing, evidencing his belief in the staff and students rather than casting aspersion of its past performance. He tirelessly walks the walls with his bullhorn: admonishing, praising, and cajoling." Barbara Simmons, Media Specialist, Southern High School, Durham, N. C.

"A principal on a mission." Richard Riley, U. S. Education Secretary

Printed in the United States
21769LVS00005B/91-141